GO Canada

The Coming Boom in the Toronto Stock Market & How to Profit from It

Robert J. Haber

Fenn Publishing Company Ltd.

Fenn Publishing Company Ltd.

Go Canada: The Coming Boom in the Toronto Stock Market and How to Profit from It

A Fenn Publishing Book / First Published in 2010

Copyright 2010 © Robert J. Haber

Library and Archives Canada Cataloguing in Publication Data available upon request.

The publisher gratefully acknowledges the support of the Canada Council for the Arts and the Ontario Arts Council for its publishing program. We acknowledge the support of the Government of Ontario through the Ontario Media Development Corporation's Ontario Book Initiative.

 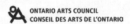 Conseil des Arts du Canada   Canada Council for the Arts   ONTARIO ARTS COUNCIL   CONSEIL DES ARTS DE L'ONTARIO

We acknowledge the financial support of the Government of Canada through the Canada Book Fund (CBF) for our publishing activities. Care has been taken to trace ownership of copyright material in this book and to secure permissions. The publishers will gladly receive any information that will enable them to rectify errors or omissions.

Fenn Publishing Company Ltd.
Bolton, Ontario, Canada
www.hbfenn.com

Text design: Jack Steiner

Printed and bound in Canada

10 11 12 13 14 5 4 3 2 1

FSC
MIX
Paper
FSC™ C016245

DEDICATION

To my dearest Marcy, Marisa and Adam: thanks for being a big part of this journey.

ACKNOWLEDGEMENTS

After you read this book, you will realize that the many successes I have enjoyed are the result of a strong team. I mention many of my "team" by name in the book. For those I couldn't include, please accept my thanks for hard work and great investment ideas. I would especially like to add John Wilson and Bob Murch to that group for their friendly and valuable assistance over many years.

I also would like to acknowledge Jade Colbert of Colborne Communications, an efficient and valuable editor, and book designer Jack Steiner, especially for creating the charts. Most of all, I need to acknowledge the completely invaluable assistance of Andrew Trimble. Andrew, a gifted financial writer, was instrumental in researching, organizing and composing. In many ways, I consider Andrew a co-author.

Contents

"Speculators buy the trend, investors are in for the long haul.
They are a different breed of cats."
REMINISCENCES OF A STOCK OPERATOR, EDWIN LEFÈVRE, 1923

W hen it comes to investing, there's a large amount of information that goes into any decision.

Some of that information comes from fundamental research you do looking into a company, its competitors and the industry it inhabits. Some comes from technical and quant analysts who study charts looking for relationships in numbers, assessing the playing field, and figuring out where the market has been in order to determine where it will go. Other information comes from the managers running the companies where you're thinking of investing. Sentiment is also important. How do investors feel right now? Do they hate stocks, love them, or are they somewhere in between? Still other information comes from the people you work with: portfolio managers and analysts. We share ideas all the time. In meetings, on elevators, in hallways and over lunch. Other sources of information can come from a neighbour, an acquaintance and the media. That could be newspapers, magazines, books, the web or the television shows my kids watch.

Over time, pieces of information may come together to form an investment thesis, or what I like to call a mosaic. You're not always conscious that the mosaic is forming. Your mind keeps arranging and re-arranging different bits of information, adding and subtracting pieces as you go until a picture forms. It may take weeks months, or even years to complete the mosaic. Sometimes it never comes, or something happens to destroy it. Other times the mosaic appears crystal clear.

The latter is what happened in the case of the following story. You'll see how pieces of information came together to form the mosaic that tells me that over the next 10 years, the Toronto Stock Exchange is going to boom lead by oil, gold, and agriculture. The pieces started to appear as early as 1998, but the picture wasn't complete until 2007 or thereabouts—just before the financial crisis, which, as you will see, only strengthened my vision of the mosaic.

You'll also find out about the 20-odd members of the Canadian equity investment group called Team Canada. When I got the opportunity to become Fidelity Canada's Chief Investment Officer, there was no team. You'll discover how it came together and the bold choices these people made when they joined. Many had to move to Boston to become part of Team Canada years before it relocated to Toronto and Montreal. So part of the boom story belongs to them.

And you. Whether you make your own investment decisions or you employ someone to make the decisions for you, I think you deserve to hear about Canada's promise. I don't know if my being American helps, but when I look at what's going on in the world and I look north, I can't help thinking how lucky you guys are. The global balance of power is shifting and Canada is sitting in the sweet spot. And the Toronto Stock Exchange is at the centre of the sweet spot. I'm not sure enough Canadians recognize this. That's something I hope to change in the following pages.

Because this book is written for investors, it will be of little use to traders and speculators. I have no stock recommendations. I have no Top 10 lists, nor do I have a set timetable telling you when to buy or sell except to say we've seen the first act of a three-act play. The first act ended with a fire-in-the-theatre type intermission— the financial crisis—in 2008. We're seeing the curtain rise on the second act now, and this is going to last awhile. About 10 years. This isn't a CNBC flavour-of-the-month segment or some flailing-chicken investment opportunity that has to be taken advantage of today and sold tomorrow.

A lot of time and thought is wasted on those things because the business press caters to the traders and speculators. It doesn't mean you should ignore it, but you've got to put it into context. Ask yourself if it fits a bigger mosaic. There are entire forests felled talking about these "events." Every day, analysts fill the airwaves on TV and columns in newspapers writing about things like the hottest TV show or the newest fashion at The Gap. These do affect stock prices, but the effect tends to be ephemeral and it's tough to catch unless you are a trader or a speculator. My focus with this book is investors who are looking for something longer than a three-month trade. The stuff we're talking about here is going to change, *is* changing the face of the planet, and by definition, it's going to happen slowly.

When I was a kid, the "Made in Japan" label was something we joked about. Now, 40 years later, I hear people of all ages proudly proclaim, "I've got a Sony, I've got a Mitsubishi and I've got a Lexus" and they covet this stuff. In the late 1980s, when Hyundai started to export cars from Korea to North America, it was the butt of jokes but now people say, "Oh, wow that's a nice car" and Hyundai has become a leading automaker taking significant market share in the U.S. In China, they're making all sorts of high-tech gadgets, and no one seems to mind that. That's a big change in terms of perception, and it's the kind of story you'll never see on the 24/7 business channel. It's too slow. It just creeps up on us and becomes every day. Just recently, I had to replace my washer and dryer. Next thing I know, I have a Korean washer and dryer. Unthinkable 15 years ago.

That's why I like charts that go way back: 50, 100, even a 1,000 years in some cases. I'll introduce you to a few of these along the way. I like them for two reasons. First, they're simple. A quick look and you can see where we are today versus yesterday. It's hard for people with this deluge of info, to find a few indicators that only talk to them once in a while, because they feel like they have to know why something happens every day. Some people look at certain indicators and say, "It's 2.06 today but yesterday it was 2.07. Oh! Sell your whole portfolio." Old charts, on the other hand, give out a signal once or twice in your lifetime. That's really when you ought to be listening, because most of the other stuff is just noise and open to interpretation, which is the second reason I like old charts. They show you what happened and when as a statement of fact. They're not really open to interpretation.

The glue that holds the pieces of my boom mosaic in place are fact-based. This isn't some theory. The changes taking place in the world today that put the Toronto Stock Exchange in the most favourable position among G8 stock markets are measurable. The data is there. So what could go wrong? I suppose I could write page after page detailing possibilities and still come up short for some people. Similarly, I'm sure there will be readers who, after the boom is over, point to my 30,000-point target and say I'm off by a couple hundred or even a thousand points. I can't help that. In my mind, the only way this can go wrong is if you're anything less than a long-term investor. Yes, the TSX will fall from time to time over the next five to 10 years. Yes, there will be instances when the index will trade sideways. And yes, there is a chance that we could witness another 2008 or some variation thereof. But as long as you're in this for the long term, you're going to come out ahead. No one can predict the future with complete certainty, but the confluence of events around the world gives me confidence the boom is on and it has legs.

You just need to look at the world through a different lens to see the boom coming, and I emphasize the word *look*. Because I think the world is too focused on the U.S. and its daily machinations—housing prices, debt, health care—and, as a result, many people are missing the real story driving the world today. If you step back and change the lens with which you are viewing the world, I think you'll see the U.S. is no longer the centre of the universe. The sooner people come to grips with that, the sooner they'll recognize opportunities available in Canada.

That's something I recognized many years ago. Whether you see the same mosaic is up to you, because it is, after all, my view. It isn't Fidelity's, nor is it Team Canada's. It's Bob Haber's. The same goes for the way I invest and the research methods I employ. They belong to me. That's why I ask you to make up your own mind. My aim with this book is simply to increase your awareness.

And to do that, we turn to Chapter One.

PART ONE

The Coming Boom

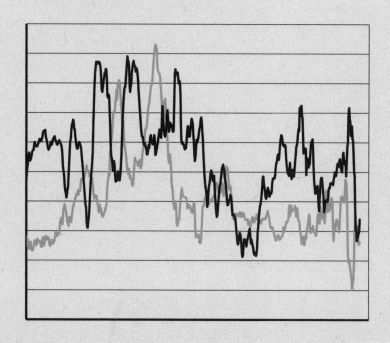

CHAPTER ONE

A period like no other

"One high-rise a day and one boulevard every three days."
UNOFFICIAL SLOGAN OF SHENZHEN, CHINA

I've got a cottage about a two and a half hours from my home in Boston. It's in the middle of nowhere. The place is special to my family and it's set in beautiful country. Lakes, trees and forests for miles. I had some work done on the cottage at the end of 2009 and I got to talking to the guy doing the hammering. When he's not busy fixing things, he's a full-time custom-home builder. He's seen many building cycles, having been in business more than 25 years. I like him. He's a very bright guy. His name is Jim.

When I spoke to Jim, he was lamenting how, for the first time in his life, the building business had fallen off a cliff yet the price of materials hadn't come down. Every other time we've had a recession, poor economy or, in this case, a huge housing collapse, so falls the price of copper, steel, wood and all the other stuff Jim uses to build homes. But that hasn't happened this time around, so a new home that Jim builds isn't any less expensive than an existing one. His costs haven't come down far enough. This is hurting his business.

What's different this time around? The answer lies thousands of miles away in a handful of countries where they're buying the stuff Jim needs to build houses. Demand from these countries drives up the prices of Jim's building materials. Copper, steel, lumber, concrete—it's going to the Chinas, Indias, Brazils, Russias, Indonesias and Vietnams of the world.

This tells me something's going on in the world. Something that's changing the neighbourhood, so to speak—the world's neighbourhood. Over the course of hundreds of years, each generation has witnessed one, sometimes two predominant investment themes that have reshaped the neighbourhood. If you were born in the 1500s, it was the printing press, in the 1870s, railroads, and in the 1920s, cars. Most recently, it was the Internet. Just think about how it's changed your life over the past 20 years. Think how many hours a day you spend on the web, how you transact, communicate with others and so on. It changed the neighbourhood, just as the car created the suburbs, the printing press democratized societies and railroads opened the West.

Today, the rapid industrialization of the developing world is changing the neighbourhood. It's stories of Jim, it's stories about TVs, iPods, computers and everything else that comes from China instead of the U.S. And it's about Canada thriving even when the U.S. sneezes. It used to be if the U.S. sneezed, Canada caught a cold. That's no longer the case. Sure, the market went down in Canada in 2008 and there were a few moments of fear because of the prior pattern, but you look at the two countries now and the U.S. is struggling to create one private sector job while Canada is creating lots of jobs, the American housing market is flatlining while it's surging in Canada. The situation's the same when you compare the two countries' financial markets. That's because Canada is rich in many of the commodities that developing countries need to keep their red-hot economies stoked. This is creating unprecedented growth opportunities for the Toronto Stock Exchange due to its heavy concentration in things that would hurt if you dropped them on your foot. It's been said the S&P/TSX is made up of four sectors: financials, mining, energy and everything else. Take a closer look and you'll notice the TSX has the most investable assets in the world when it comes to gold, oil and agricultural fertilizers. Moreover, there are many more stocks in other categories that are both directly and indirectly affected by these three drivers. And as the world gets larger, richer and hungrier, it's going to be great for the Canadian economy and the Toronto Stock Exchange.

Yes, the neighbourhood is changing. The balance of power has shifted and China is the leader. It has been transformed into the locomotive of the world economy. Just look to its GDP growth. Real gross domestic product growth, the measure of all goods and services produced in a country is a key barometer of a country's economic strength. Between 2000 and 2010, China posted a world-beating average growth rate of about 10%.[1] In the first decade of the new millenium, China has contributed about 15% of world GDP growth,[2] and that figure is expected to double over the next 10 years.[3] In the first quarter 2006, China's 11.1% growth contributed more to global GDP than the United States, which was a first.[4] Although China's GDP is still smaller than the U.S.'s by quite a bit when it comes to investing, the change of a variable is oftentimes more important than the absolute size. It is the change in China and Asian growth relative to the old world that is the key variable.*

China now ranks as the world's number one exporter,[5] the world's biggest automaker[6] and its largest energy consumer.[7] More broadly, the Chinese economy has grown in size to overtake the major European countries

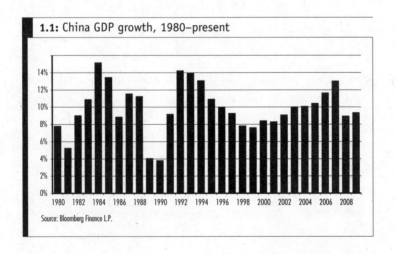

1.1: China GDP growth, 1980–present

Source: Bloomberg Finance L.P.

---

*Many rightly question the data upon which China and developing countries rely on to arrive at official statistics. The overall trend is what matters, and the relative change from one number to the next.

starting with the U.K., France and Italy in 2006 and Germany in 2007.[8] Most recently, China leapfrogged Japan as the second largest economy in the world according to GDP output in the second quarter 2010.[9]

Three other countries are following the same trajectory as China: Brazil, Russia and India. Both India and Brazil are poised to join the G7, the rich club of the seven most industrialized countries, within the next 10 years based on current GDP growth.* Collectively, they are referred to as the BRICs—a term coined by Goldman Sachs in a 2001 research paper.† In the paper, Goldman suggested that the BRICs would make up more than 10% of the world's GDP by the end of 2010. At the end of 2009, they contributed 28% of world GDP growth.[10] Brazil, India and Russia are now in the US$1 trillion club, which puts them among or near the top 10 in the world.[11]

Lumped together, the BRICs' share of world GDP is impressive. And they continue to carve up larger slices of the pie. According to 2010 Goldman estimates, the BRICs are projected to account for a third of the global economy and contribute half of all global GDP growth by 2020. By 2018, they will have overtaken the U.S. on an individual country basis. China will deliver more to global

---

*The G7 countries are France, Germany, Italy, Japan, U.K., U.S. and Canada. When people refer to the G8 it includes Russia, which joined in 1997.
†Goldman Sachs deserves credit for being one of the first to identify, research and analyze the rise of the BRICs. Research documents related to the BRICs are posted at their website: www2.goldmansachs.com.

growth than the G3 by 2020. India and Russia will, in the meantime, grow become individually larger than Spain, Canada, or Italy by 2020.[12] Goldman is quick to point out that much can happen to these projections over the next 20 years. Personally, I see the value in the ranking coming from the trend behind the forecasted placements rather than the certainty of an explicit pecking order.

Regardless of who comes first, second or third, there is a dramatic shift underway in the balance of economic power. Where it will end may be open to debate, but the world is changing. When you bundle the BRICs with other industrializing countries across the globe (Indonesia, Malaysia, the Philippines, Vietnam, Mexico, Turkey, Egypt, Nigeria, Bangladesh, Peru, Chile), they are now responsible for two-thirds of global growth according to the IMF. In the 1970s, their share was about half that.

Brazil, Russia, India and China were among the five countries to take on the most infrastructure projects with private participation from 1990 to 2004. China is the leader with more than 400 completed; Brazil took second with nearly 300, while Russia placed third with about 200 projects under its belt. India placed fifth, just behind Argentina. China alone was responsible for 15% of total projects.[13] A wide range of commodities are feeling the impact of these billions spent on infrastructure.

In the area of base metals, BRIC consumption has shown steady growth since 2000 with China leading the way. For the past five years, China has consumed the most refined copper, primary aluminum, nickel, slab zinc (30% of global demand), and lead (25% of global demand) of any country in the world.[14] It's a similar story for industrial metals: China's share of world demand for refined zinc, nickel, lead, aluminum and copper has increased twofold since 2000.[15] Of the five industrial metals, the demand for copper is the best predictor of economic growth because it's a key element for infrastructure development. That ability to predict the ups and downs in the economy is what has earned the metal its "Dr. Copper" moniker—*doctor* meant in a PhD in economics sort of way. Buildings, houses, factories, cities, cars and machines are copper-intensive due to their electrical wiring. There is even greater demand for nickel, which is primarily used for making stainless steel and corrosive-resistant plating. The electrical, automotive and hardware industries use zinc, another hot commodity, to make die castings. Meanwhile, aluminum is used for a wide range of industrial applications and manufactured goods, including autos, and consumer goods, such as cooking utensils.

Although many Canadian companies are benefiting and will continue to benefit from the surge in commodity demand, the companies with the brightest futures reside in the gold, oil and agricultural sectors. The reasons are many and I'll deal with the specifics in the chapters focussing on each of these industries, but at its essence, the coming boom comes down to this: there simply isn't enough supply to meet current demand, it will be years before meaningful production comes on stream to meet that demand, and the Toronto Stock Exchange is poised to take advantage of this supply shortfall.

Gold has already been on a tear with BRIC gold consumption up strongly over the past 10 years. Since 2002, the four countries have been responsible for nearly a quarter of total world demand for the precious metal, and a large number of other developing countries have been active buyers.[16] Gold holds such potential because—unlike with other base, industrial and precious metals—global gold production has not been this low since 2000, producing a major demand and supply imbalance.

Oil faces a similar crunch with China being the biggest user. It was in 1985 as a Fidelity energy analyst that I noticed China was consuming 2 million barrels of crude oil per day, and even at 2 million barrels, Chinese demand wasn't a major factor in world markets. That figure stayed in my head for years. When I checked again in 2000, I noticed the figure had jumped to 4 million barrels. Now they're at 8 million. Overall, China's share of world oil consumption has risen by three-quarters over the past 10 years. Of all the oil the world consumes in a day, China burns up 8.2% of it. Oil consumption is also notably on the rise in Brazil, India, Russia and the rest of the developing countries trailing in their wake. But with production levels dropping in oil fields around the world, fresh concerns about deepwater drilling stemming after the Gulf oil spill, and not nearly enough discoveries of new, untapped wells, oil finds itself in the same demand and supply imbalance as gold.

Meanwhile, a number of factors—rising global populations, increased demand for better, higher-protein diets, and the accelerating loss of arable land suitable for growing crops—are compromising the world's ability to feed itself. Combined, the BRICs consume 36% of the world's wheat, 32% of its corn and 37% of its soybeans.[17] In addition to stocking pantries, grains also feed surging livestock populations. A third of the corn grown in the world never reaches the dinner table at all, instead going to the production of ethanol. During the next 20 years, food production may need to rise 50% to meet demand.[18]

In addition to the reality of current commodity demand, I am certain of future demand because we've watched many countries—the U.S., Canada, Great Britain, France, Germany, Japan, and so on—traverse the paths to industrialization over the past 400 years.

We can, as a result, intuit that the destination will be the same for the current up-and-comers, a point brought home by the many similarities shared between today's industrializing countries and those of previous generations. The first and perhaps most important commonality among them is the vision or goal of industrialization. In order for a country to move from an agrarian to an industrial society, country leadership must have what's been described as the "will to economize."[19]

1.2: The conceptual S curve—the underlying economic engine

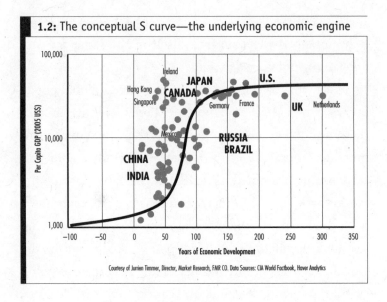

Courtesy of Jurrien Timmer, Director, Market Research, FMR CO. Data Sources: CIA World Factbook, Haver Analytics

This "will" can be stated publicly or simply supported by action. Deng Xiaoping made it clear to the world in 1974 that China was moving from a centrally planned to a market-based economy. Another important step was the country's inclusion in the World Trade Organization. Russia, on the other hand, took its bold step forward by turning its back on communism and started privatizing formerly state-run enterprises in the 1990s. India announced reforms starting in 1991, and in the same decade, Brazil accelerated the apparatus necessary to "economize." For example, the Brazilian government re-affirmed its energy independence through the use of sugar ethanol and the opening of major offshore oil leases.

The second crucial step is to establish the apparatus

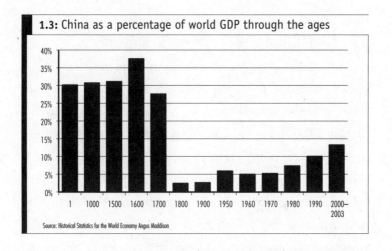

1.3: China as a percentage of world GDP through the ages

Source: Historical Statistics for the World Economy Angus Maddison

necessary for industrialization. Countries must be willing to undertake fundamental changes in the structure of their economies and institutions to move from planned economies to market-based ones.[20] Consider the Chinese miracle. Throughout history, China has produced some of the most innovative, most ingenious people on earth. In fact, China's rise on the global stage is more of a resurgence than it is an incarnation.

China led the world in GDP for almost 2,000 years until communism took root. It wasn't until the government altered land policies, adjusted tariffs, changed laws and broke away from its Maoist roots that we saw the seeds of industrialization take root.* Other important enablers are

---

*When people ask what industrialization means, there is no single answer, no single combination of factors and no single scholar who can agree on a buttoned-down definition. For me, the key proof point of industrialization is the lifting of masses of people out of poverty.

public funds and the welcoming of foreign capital, which have both helped other countries industrialize.

A large portion of the infrastructure in the U.S.—canals, bridges, railways—was financed by bonds sold to Londoners and Europeans. U.S. state governments provided land grants to colleges, railways and a long list of other beneficiaries to pave the way for U.S. industrialization.[21] In Japan, radical land and labour reforms along with the elimination of the industrial monopolistic conglomerates called *zaibatsu* led to the country's industrialization and pre-eminence after the Second World War.[22] The four-lane (and increasingly, six-lane) highway linking India's four largest cities—Delhi, Kolkata, Chennai and Mumbai—wouldn't have been possible without government sponsorship. Completed at the end of the 1990s, the so-called Golden Quadrilateral highway project added 3,635 miles to India's road systems after a 50-year period that saw the addition of only 334 miles of four-lane roads.[23] In each of the above instances, changes in economic activities were led by fundamental changes in laws, institutions and prior work practices.

As many similarities as there may be between the BRICs' current journey and the development of today's industrialized economies before them, there are also unprecedented differences. These differences warrant special attention because of their impact on the investment opportunity before us.

The first difference is that we have never seen

industrialization on this large a scale. The BRICs' combined population tallies to 2.5–3 billion. That's 40% of the planet's population—6.8 billion people in four countries—according to the U.S. Census Bureau. This is massive. Never before has such a large number of people graduated from the underdeveloped to the developing world. To date, the most populated country to industrialize was Japan. When it started down the industrialization path in 1945, the nation's population stood at about 70 million. The population of the United States in the 1880s, the years when its major industrialization phase was in full-bloom, was about 50 million and when Great Britain started to turn the corner in 1780, it contained about 10 million people. Combined, that works out to about 130 million people living in these countries as they started to industrialize. Now we're talking about 20 times that number of people living in the BRICs alone, quite aside from all the other developing countries. This means potentially 20 times the impact on demand.

The second unprecedented aspect of this massive transition is really a sub-point to the first: these changes are happening concurrently. I mentioned the big three—the U.S., Great Britain and Japan—and identified the various dates when they industrialized. Historically, the pattern of industrialization is one where a single country jumps out in front, takes centre stage and grabs the headlines. Great Britain was the first, the United States, second, and Japan, the third. The GDP and per capita income growth rates of these countries rose steadily, and each of these countries had their time in the sun when they lead the world in terms of growth. The same is happening today. What's different is that it's happening in lockstep, simultaneously among four countries, not just one as was the historical norm. This means that this boom is more diversified than booms previous, so if one country stalls or hits a rough patch economically, politically or socially, there are others to pick up the slack. This boom isn't a one-hit wonder. Further, these four economies are additive and complementary as they industrialize. Brazil is the farmer, Russia, the gas station attendant, China, the factory worker and India, the back-office services provider. This diversification broadens the impact of the BRICs' commodities-driven demands across a wider spectrum of goods, particularly in the area of agriculture.

A third departure from the historical norms of industrialization is the speed with which this set of industrialization is occurring. Scholars peg the genesis of Great Britain's industrialization as far back as 1700—a full 100 or so years before the country could officially be labeled as industrialized. The United States was a bit faster with industrialization, starting around 1800 and coming into full bloom about 1880. Japan saw its radical transformation occur from about 1945 to 1970. Today, we look at the BRICs and see China's bold industrialization starting in the late 1970s shortly after Chinese leader Deng Xiaoping announced his liberalization plans. For

Russia, the rise of glasnost, perestroika and its move to a free-market economy in 1991 was the big turning point. Brazil and India are now hitting their stride. So the pace of industrialization seems to be accelerating. Of course we will only know well after the fact the true pace, but we do know the BRICs are intent to get it done "yesterday."

I've focused the majority of my comments on the BRICs, and China as its leading light, for good reason. They are the biggest, the most influential and have taken the greatest strides along the path to industrialization. But for every China there is an Indonesia, a Taiwan, a Philippines or a Vietnam. For every Russia, an East Germany, a Poland and a Hungary. All of Eastern Europe is starting down this path in one form or another. The same can be said of Chile, Peru and Argentina in the Western hemisphere. And in Asia, the list includes Indonesia, Taiwan, Korea, the Philippines and Vietnam. All those countries are in the game now.

Take Vietnam for example. Just 15 years ago it was a closed society. Now I'm looking at my Nike sneakers and on the tongue of my shoe it says "Made in Vietnam." You could say, "Well, Vietnam, who cares?" But how many people live in Vietnam? It's close to 100 million, which is three times Canada's population. And if Vietnam is making sneakers now, it's a sure bet they'll be making other things down the road. In five or 10 years some of the Vietnamese will have motorbikes, they may have cars or something else that they don't have now. To me there's something happening in the world that's more compelling than all the numbers, all the estimates and the projections. It's about human beings aspiring to have a better life. That's easy to believe in. It's what our parents wanted for us, and what we want for our children. Why would it be different anywhere else in the world?

These are the factors that make this period like no other. The scope, speed and magnitude of this industrialization is unprecedented. But the rise of the BRICs and their overarching need for commodities is only half the story, for if the world was producing everything these rising economies needed, demand by itself would not be enough to create a boom. No, the other side of the equation, supply—or in this case, undersupply—is just as important. To better understand the supply side of the story, we need to turn back the clock to the actions of Paul Volcker as Federal Reserve Board Chairman in the early 1980s. Little did Volcker know that his actions 30 years ago would unleash a set of consequences setting us up for the boom today.

The U.S. Federal Reserve, or the Fed, was created the day before Christmas Eve, 1913. Any bill passed on Christmas is one intended to be hidden from the light of day, and that's certainly true of the bill that created the Fed. That's because the Fed was partly a creature of J.P. Morgan and John D. Rockefeller—the two richest people in the world—whose representatives met on J.P. Morgan's private island off the coast of South Carolina called, of all things, Jekyll Island. They invited 15 or 20 of their top banker henchmen to write the Fed bill. It was all very secret. Participants were not allowed to use last names or discuss their modes of travel and there could be no paper trail, no bills, no railroad tickets.

These guys sensed the time was ripe for change. The year before, Woodrow Wilson had become president championing something called the Progressive Movement. Up until then, it was Republican after Republican in office, but in '12, Wilson snuck in for a couple of reasons. One was the Republicans split the ticket that year between William Howard Taft and Teddy Roosevelt after the latter created his own party. The second reason Wilson was elected lay in his Democratic platform promising more government to help the people, more power to the unions and his pledge to break up the trusts. So Morgan and Rockefeller seized the opportunity to convince Wilson and the Progressive Movement that the Fed's creation would help the little guy because it would stop bank runs. Until then, bank runs were scary because there was no deposit insurance. If you put your $50 in the bank, you might have lost it. So Morgan and Rockefeller cajoled Wilson into creating the Fed and the bill was rammed through on Christmas Eve. The first head of the bank was, surprise, surprise, one of Rockefeller's sons-in-law and Morgan's first lieutenant, Senator Nelson Aldrich.

What really motivated Morgan and Rockefeller to create a central bank was self-interest. The country was really growing at the time and bank runs were disrupting growth potential, which hurt these guys in the pocketbook. In 1907 there had been a run on the bank and J.P. Morgan and his company, working with the federal government, had to inject tens of millions of dollars into the banks, stock exchanges, and even New York City bonds to avert a complete, systemic collapse. John D. Rockefeller contributed roughly $10 million to the cause as well.

Both Morgan and Rockefeller were worried the next bank run could wipe them out. So, they figured, why not socialize the risk? They sensed Wilson and his Progressive Movement would be open to the thought, which they were. Some people think history is black and white and most figures stupid. I can tell you Morgan and Rockefeller knew exactly what they were doing. That's how the Fed was started. It wasn't popular at all. Wilson, after he retired, said the single biggest mistake he made as a politician was starting the Fed. By the way, since the Fed was created, the U.S. dollar has lost an astounding 95% of its purchasing power, which is a precursor to the money-printing actions they are taking now and a possible guide to the outcome as well.

With the Fed's creation, the U.S. was the last of the major industrialized countries to establish a central bank. One of its key priorities—to manage the nation's monetary policy in pursuit of maximum employment, stable prices and moderate long-term interest rates—is where the answers lie concerning the other half of our boom story: supply constraints.

By the mid-1970s the United States was going through a crisis of confidence. After the rip-roaring 1950s and '60s, American corporations grew lazy and complacent in contrast to their global competitors who had become increasingly agile and determined. Epitomizing the times was the spring 1979 cover of *Business Week* that showed the Statue of Liberty with a tear running down her face. The headline read "The Decline of U.S. Power." The tears shed weren't just for corporate America. The economy was in a mess. There were big bills to pay for the Vietnam War, unemployment was rising to levels not seen since the Great Depression, the U.S. dollar was plummeting in value and prices of everything were running rampant. In October 1979, the U.S. inflation rate stood at 12%, up from 8% a year earlier. The inflation plague wasn't just restricted to the United States. In Britain, France, Germany and most of the industrialized world, consumer prices were marching higher to keep pace with rising commodity costs.[24] To make matters worse, the U.S. had just been through a bruising recession from 1973 to 1975 leading to "stagflation," a term coined by a British parliamentarian to describe an extraordinary and contradictory situation: rampant inflation despite economic stagnation.

Against this backdrop, wealth around the globe looked to gold as a hedge against both inflation and a falling U.S. dollar. At the beginning of 1972, gold stood at US$46 an ounce. By the end of the year, it had hit US$64. Gold cracked US$100 an ounce the following year and after fluctuating between US$130 and US$180 an ounce from 1974 to 1977, it quickly resumed its rise. In 1978, the price hit US$244 an ounce and then doubled to US$500 in 1979. By the time the calendar flipped to January 1980, the price jumped another US$110 an ounce to US$634— in two business days. Before the month was out, gold would eventually reach its record high of US$850 an ounce. This bookended an extraordinary boom that saw the price rise from US$35 to US$850 an ounce in a period of 12 years. That represented a gain of over 30% a year for each of those dozen years outpacing inflation, which averaged 7.5% over the same period.*

If gold was the beneficial recipient of inflation, it had all commodities to thank but principally oil because oil was the biggest culprit driving inflation. In 1972, the price of crude was about US$3 a barrel. In October 1973, Syria and Egypt attacked Israel in what would become known as the Yom Kippur War. The U.S. and a host of other western countries supported Israel leading to the

---

*The preceding historical review of gold prices comes from the excellent book *The Power of Gold, The History of an Obsession*. It was an important piece of my investment mosaic, and I owe much to its author, Peter L. Bernstein, who is frequently cited in this work.

Arab oil embargo, which saw several exporting nations and Iran halt oil shipments. The result was a net loss of 4 million barrels a day through March 1974. By the end of the year, the price of oil had quadrupled to US$12 a barrel. Between 1974 and 1978, the price of crude hovered around US$13 a barrel, but by the time 1978 came to an end, oil stood at US$35 a barrel. The Iranian revolution and subsequent hostage-taking of Americans in November 1979 pushed oil to its highest price since the Second World War with crude reaching US$37 a barrel, almost US$80 a barrel in 2008 dollars.[25]

To illustrate the dominance of oil in the U.S. economy one need only look to the stock market. Using it as a proxy to tell us where people thought profits and profitability were coming from in 1981, it screamed oil. At the time, 32% of the S&P 500 stock market capitalization was in energy. It was higher in Canada. That tells you we were living in a world that revolved around oil. If a third of the U.S. stock market is in energy, that's where the profits are coming from, and that's the industry that investors expect to be the big thing. If you're someone that relies on oil to produce consumer goods, which is almost everyone, you're not held in high regard by the market because your sales and profit margins are being gobbled up by crude. You are a casualty of high oil. Conversely, if you're someone who stands to profit from rising oil—explorers, producers, drillers—the market wants to own you.

To understand how the price of oil affects producers

of consumer goods, think about something as simple as a box of Kellogg's Corn Flakes in 1981. The price of cardboard on the outside is at the highest it's ever been because the machines that produce the material run on oil. The little plastic liner that holds the cereal is made from petroleum, so it too is at the highest price it's ever been. The little bits of corn on the inside are similarly surging in price because agriculture commodities are very sensitive to oil prices. Then you've got to assemble these pieces—the box, liner, wheat—and gas up a truck to send it to the supermarket. You can see how the rising price of oil inflates commodity prices.

With prices rising, capital increasingly finds its way into commodities. Plants are built, production is ramped up and new supplies come online. Whether it's base, industrial, agriculture or energy commodities, all are attracting record sums of money to take advantage of the pricing environment. With regard to oil, billions are poured into exploration and a record number of new wells are drilled in North America and around the world. The U.S. Rotary Rig count gives us an idea of just how fast things were spinning. The rig count tracks the average number of drilling rigs being used to look for oil and gas in the United States. As you can imagine, drilling costs a lot of money, so before you set up a rig, you're going to weigh that investment against your expected return. This is why the count is a useful measure of the industry's confidence in the future: if you aren't confident in your return on investment, you aren't going to drill. At the end of the oil embargo in 1974, the rig count was below 1,500 in the U.S. It rose to 2,000 in 1979 and by 1982 it was above 3,000.[26]

Gold exploration and extraction also got a lot of attention in the late 1970s and early '80s. Global gold production fell by over 25% between 1975 and 1980, but with ever-higher prices for gold, the world started panning again,[27] and not just in typical gold countries like South Africa. For the first time since the 1840s San Francisco gold rush, U.S. gold companies pulled out their maps and aggressively set out to find new deposits. It was a similar story in Canada, Australia, Brazil and China.

With runaway inflation, a falling U.S. dollar and growing unemployment as his walk-on music, Volcker steps onto the scene as Chairman of the Federal Reserve. Appointed by then-president Jimmy Carter, Volker got the job of getting America back on track. He acted quickly. Within five months of his appointment, he hit the brakes on money supply. He ratcheted up the prime rate on business loans at large banks from 11.5% in mid-1979 to 20% in early April 1980.[28] The prime rate, or the rate that banks lend to their most creditworthy customers, hit 21.5% the same year. With Volcker hitting the breaks hard, he not only killed inflation—it plummeted to 3.2% by 1983—he also killed the boom in commodities. As a student of the market, which I consider myself to be, there are long cycles that run through markets and economies.

Volker's efforts to bring inflation to a halt marked the end of the last great commodity boom, particularly in the gold and oil sectors.

In the U.S., sky-high interest rates choked off any and all forms of business expansion, tipping the economy back into recession. Companies were no longer building plants, hiring people or reinvesting in their businesses. Anything and everything commodity related fell through the floor as just about every sector of the U.S. economy ground to a halt in light of the cost of borrowing. American construction workers were losing jobs by the thousands. Farmers watched as their properties were foreclosed, leading to widespread protests, including a tractor blockading of the Eccles Building, home to the Federal Reserve, in Washington, D.C. Farm Aid, the 1985 benefit concert to raise money for family farms, was another sign of the times. Ironically, the huge amount of capital invested during the commodity boom in gold and oil discovery and extraction was beginning to bear fruit at the same time as both commodities were dropping in price due to slowing global growth, waning inflation fears and a rising U.S. dollar. Between 1980 and 1986, non-OPEC oil production increased to 10 million barrels a day but it was selling for only half the price compared to five years earlier.[29] World gold production, which increased 25% from 39.2 million ounces to 49.3 ounces over the same period, was being sold for US$350 an ounce, a far cry from the US$850 it fetched in January 1980.[30] This was a classic case of supply rising to meet demand. From this example we can come away with two important points. Point one is time: when successful, it takes years to find, extract and process both gold and oil before they come to market. Point two is that point one assumes that efforts to discover new gold and oil sources will indeed be successful.

The supply picture kept getting uglier for commodities. Ten years later, the fall of the Iron Curtain unleashed enormous stockpiles of commodities from former Communist countries. The release of these stockpiles that had never found their way to market in the Western World was a big event because you're already into this cycle of disinflation and then you add to it with huge inventories. The addition to supply had to be absorbed, so prices fell further, below and beyond what was thought possible at the time. Commodity producers got the message and opted not to increase capacity, not to put money into further development projects. This added another 10 years of decline.

This was the precipice Canadian commodities fell from for the better part of 20 years. The bellwether Reuters Commodity Research Bureau (CRB) index of commodities futures—a basket of 19 commodities divided into four like groups—stood at 900 in 1981, deflated for CPI. In 2001, the real CRB stood at 220.

That's the long cycle of disinflation. The process started with Fed Chairman Volcker's ethic of high interest rates and reduced money supply, and it was aided and abetted

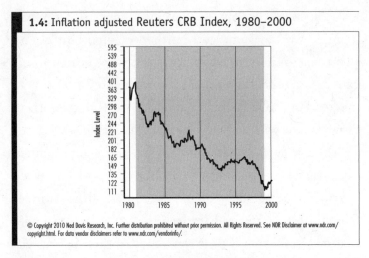

1.4: Inflation adjusted Reuters CRB Index, 1980–2000

© Copyright 2010 Ned Davis Research, Inc. Further distribution prohibited without prior permission. All Rights Reserved. See NDR Disclaimer at www.ndr.com/copyright.html. For data vendor disclaimers refer to www.ndr.com/vendorinfo/.

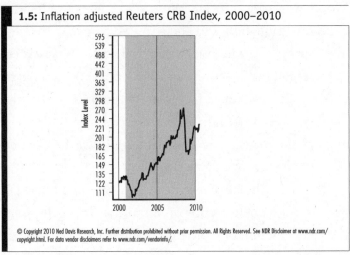

1.5: Inflation adjusted Reuters CRB Index, 2000–2010

© Copyright 2010 Ned Davis Research, Inc. Further distribution prohibited without prior permission. All Rights Reserved. See NDR Disclaimer at www.ndr.com/copyright.html. For data vendor disclaimers refer to www.ndr.com/vendorinfo/.

along the way by the fall of the Iron Curtain. It wasn't a friendly period for the Canadian market. Sharply reduced capital spending in commodity-related fields, extractive industries and the big industrial companies were the orders of the day. Commodity companies, browbeaten by investors and quarter after quarter of falling earnings, no longer invested in productive capacity. They weren't building new oil fields or exploring for new mines because they didn't expect a great return on investment and their shareholders were telling them, "That'd be crazy. Every time the price goes up a couple of bucks you put on another bit of supply and you guys kill the whole cycle again."

So what does that mean? If you're involved in industries that are extracting and producing raw industrials, you're in a tough business. A tough, capital-intensive, unglamorous business. So if you were stuck in the cycle of disinflation in the 1980s and '90s, you didn't invest. Why would you? You'd be looking at ever-declining rates of return. And this cycle didn't last for a year or two. It lasts for two decades. As a result, we have dramatically underinvested in virtually anything commodity related. In fact, we've reduced supply. Look at the number of companies in these extractive industries that existed 30 years ago and have since been consolidated and shut down.

All of a sudden, we're in a situation where we've reduced supply for 20 years but there's this new, unanticipated surge in demand gathering force. The result is a major imbalance. You pass an inflection point and you're into the next cycle. This is the set-up for the supply side of the boom. The supply side is positively impacting Canada in two ways. The first is the reflation in commodity prices, which we started to see in 2001, 2002 and up until we reached the financial crisis in 2008, when we saw the Reuters CRB Energy, Spot Metals and Grain Indexes jump 299%, 258% and 187%, respectively.

Rebounding commodity prices helped drive S&P/ TSX to an 88% return over the same period of time, which is the second positive. In fact, Canada outpaced all G8 industrialized countries' stock markets, including those of the U.S., U.K. and France, and it did it largely on the strength of the gold, oil and agricultural sectors.

Gold, oil, agriculture: these are sectors that don't really exist in the U.S. or European markets. That's Canada's connection to the boom. No other market—perhaps with the exception of Australia—has the exposure Canada does to these sectors. What will the boom look like? A slow, steady build in the Toronto Stock Exchange from its present level, which at writing is about 11,000 points. Over time, the TSX will deliver an average growth rate of 10% a year, as it, the Dow and other exchanges have done for the past 100 years. I expect that trend to continue for the next eight to 10 years taking us to about 18,000 points. The remaining push will come from boom overexuberance. During the Internet bubble, the market was overbought—*overbought* meaning the market was trading above its long-term return trendline. The Internet bubble saw the market overbought to its highest point ever—50%—as illustrated by the big, last spike in the chart. At the 11,000-point level, the TSX is currently 20% oversold. I think we'll revisit the 50% territory again.

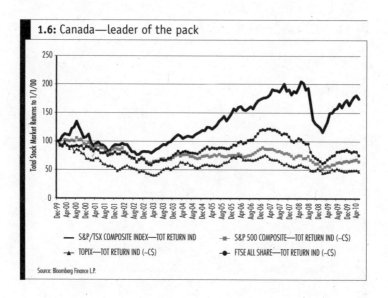

1.6: Canada—leader of the pack

— S&P/TSX COMPOSITE INDEX—TOT RETURN IND ■ S&P 500 COMPOSITE—TOT RETURN IND (–C$)
▲ TOPIX—TOT RETURN IND (–C$) ● FTSE ALL SHARE—TOT RETURN IND (–C$)

Source: Bloomberg Finance L.P.

In fact, I think we have a chance of blowing past 50% overbought. The one hiccup in the coming boom was the 2008 financial crisis. But if you're viewing this through the same lens as I am, you'll see that the period just before the crisis was but the first act of a three-act play. We've had a long, tough intermission, you know, a kind of fire-in-the-theatre intermission. But acts two and three promise to be pretty exciting because the BRICs and other developing countries have huge needs. The demand from China, India, Brazil and all those other places isn't stopping; it isn't going away. It may slacken from time to time, such as China's economy did in the second and third quarters of 2010 as they moved to cool their red-hot housing market and overall growth. But even with China tapping the brakes, its growth rate remains many multiples above that

1.7: Trendline of the Toronto stock market

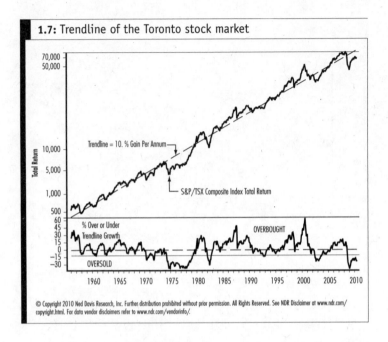

© Copyright 2010 Ned Davis Research, Inc. Further distribution prohibited without prior permission. All Rights Reserved. See NDR Disclaimer at www.ndr.com/copyright.html. For data vendor disclaimers refer to www.ndr.com/vendorinfo/.

of the U.S. and Japan. Worries about the old countries of Europe and their public debt problems will not stop the reordering of international power and the ascendancy of the Chinese consumer. So although I can't tell you when China will be consuming 10 or 15 million barrels of oil per from its current 8 billion, I know they're driving toward it. And Canadians are in the enviable and unique position to take advantage of it. You have a front-row seat to the most forceful long-term investment theme to emerge this decade. In the following chapters, we will see why gold, oil and agriculture are the deserving leading players in the boom.

Gold

"The death of gold"

FINANCIAL TIMES OP-ED PIECE, DECEMBER 13, 1997

Fidelity Investments has many offices throughout Boston and the world but in 1999 the centre of the Team Canada Equity Group's universe was 100 Federal Street in downtown Boston. The building is just south of the Old State House and a five-minute walk to the inner harbour, site of the 1773 Boston Tea Party.

We occupied the fifteenth floor, but we had plenty of company above and below. In all, 100 Federal Street housed Fidelity's equity investors, analysts and research groups on six floors. The fourteenth was home to the high-income, emerging markets and international groups; the sixteenth floor was all spit and polish conference rooms where companies would meet with us. And the seventeenth and eighteenth floors are where the U.S. portfolio managers and analysts worked.*

All told, some of the brightest, hardest working, most competitive, cerebral and analytical people in the investment world ride the elevators every morning. Each day is similar to the next: staring at screens, reading annual reports, newspapers and research reports, making

---

*Fidelity has long since departed this building.

phone calls, answering emails and of course, buying and selling stock and bonds. In the halls portfolio managers and analysts swap stock stories; in their offices, putt golf balls and sometimes on weekends, sleep there. Some of the guys—and women—are poorly dressed; others well dressed. It doesn't matter what you look like, how you speak or where you come from. Investing is about performance. If you perform, nothing else matters. But as varied as each of these people are, they share one trait: they are all problem solvers. That's what we're paid to do. Look at a situation, a company, an industry, a stock, pull it apart and solve the riddle as to whether it is a good investment or not.

The Team Canada Equity Group was something of an oddity in that the signage announcing our place had been changed a year earlier from "Canadian Equity Group" to "Team Canada Equity Group." Canada is where we were mandated to invest, but in addition to that, the team itself was mostly Canadian—by design—and a sense of pride in both the country and its hockey team made the name change a natural fit. To further assert national pride, one original team member had mounted two flags—Canada's maple leaf and Quebec's fleur-de-lis—in our meeting rooms.

It was December 1999. Two years earlier, I had asked Neil Marotta, a McGill University graduate I hired off campus, to complete and present an industry review of the gold sector. Marotta was our gold analyst and the sixth person to join Team Canada.

Marotta booked the Team Canada meeting room for his presentation over lunch. All members of the team were present, as were a couple of U.S. portfolio managers and analysts. For all in attendance, industry reviews were eagerly anticipated. The mood was light and there was a feeling of excitement in the room.

For me, industry reviews are an opportunity to step back from the day-to-day screen watching, portfolio monitoring, and newspaper, magazine and annual report reading. One of the biggest challenges for professional investors is the amount of data thrown our way. It's data that's confined to the here and now or couple of weeks down the road: earnings reports, economic releases, government initiatives and interest rate changes. Taking in all this data is like drinking from an uncapped fire hydrant. In addition to the reading, there is the calling, the questioning and the listening. Every week, the average portfolio manager will call 40 to 50 people who have dealings with a company whose stock that manager is watching. The calls are made to suppliers, distributors, wholesalers and customers to ask how they're doing with so-and-so. Are their order books full and is inventory declining?

As ubiquitous as much of this information is to the portfolio manager, we continue to drink from the fire hydrant for fear of missing a change, a figure, a new product release, anything that might alter our investment thesis or view of a stock and its prospects. In contrast, industry reviews give us a chance to look farther out. To contemplate the bigger picture in terms of an industry and a stock. To digest the overarching themes that may be taking an industry to new heights, or new depths. For Marotta, the review was an opportunity to showcase what he was made of in terms of his ability to analyze an industry and make recommendations about the companies that inhabit it or are impacted by it. With most of lunch eaten—deli sandwiches and pickles— Marotta rose.

"Good afternoon and thank you for coming," he began.

Marotta started by giving the group context on the historical price of gold. His first chart illustrated the movements in the gold price starting in 1717. With the exception of the Napoleonic Wars from 1797 to 1821, the British price didn't budge until 1914. In the U.S., the official gold price has changed only four times since 1792. Starting at US$19 a troy ounce, it was raised to US$20.67 in 1834 and, 110 years later, to US$35. In 1972, the price was raised to US$38 and then to US$42.22 in 1973.*

The relative stability behind these numbers masks a history that's far from stable. Our longing for and fascination with gold have been two of mankind's longest-running obsessions.[1] From the earliest

---

*Prices from 1883–1994, World Gold Council. Taken from Timothy Green's Historical Gold Price Table. London prices converted to US$. Prices from 1995–2008, Kitco.com, based on the London PM fix.

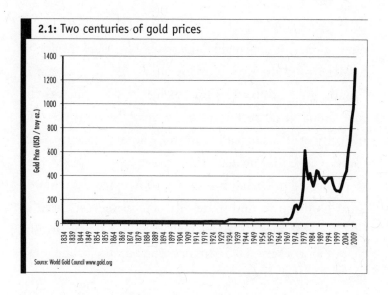

2.1: Two centuries of gold prices

Source: World Gold Council www.gold.org

civilizations—Mesopotamian, Greek, Roman, Persian, Egyptian and Chinese—people have revered, hoarded, worshipped and killed for gold. Of all the treasures taken from the earth, pillaged from conquest or pirated at sea, every society has recognized gold as having value. Familiarizing oneself with the history of gold—the role it's played in societies and their financial systems—is central to understanding the current rise in the price of the yellow metal and why it's one of the leading players in the boom before us.

Most writers on the subject of gold ascribe its value to the unique and contradictory properties it displays as a metal.[2] It's extremely dense yet malleable enough for gilding, which requires gold to be hammered paper-thin or as little as five-millionths of an inch. Gold is chemically inert, so it doesn't rust, corrode or, for that matter, wear out. In fact, it's virtually indestructible even though it has destroyed the lives of many who've tried to obtain it. Finally, gold exhibits a shine so lustrous that it was the first metal to attract the attention of humans, yet the majority of it sits gleaming in well-protected vaults never to be seen by its owners. Primitive people thought they were blessed or cursed by possessing it, explorers endured great hardship to find more of it and alchemists tried in vain to reproduce it. The history of gold is unequalled by that of any other metal, gem or stone because of the sense of value it bestows.

Not surprisingly, it became the one material we would accept for payment in lieu of goods and services. The big drawback was that each piece of gold had to be weighed and tested for purity, making for a time-consuming, cumbersome process. Coin money was invented to solve this problem. The Mesopotamians went so far as to break their gold monies into smaller denominations, calling them talents, minas and shekels. These pieces were widely accepted for trade throughout Asia Minor, in Greek cities and other settlements on the Mediterranean. The word *shekel* lives on today as a denomination of Israel's currency.[3]

Other civilizations, including the Romans, Egyptians Babylonians and Assyrians, travelled down the coinage route. As crude as the coins were in those days, the people tasked with minting them took great care to ensure each was stamped with a crest, logo or other signifying feature of the ruler of the day, and the denomination. Generally, the coins were sold on weight using a scale to determine how much they were worth. Purity, measured by carats, was also important. Pure gold equals 24 carats. If alloys are added, the gold may be described as 12 carats, 14 carats, and so on.

The practice of debasement—the mixing of other alloys into coins—was taken to a high art during Roman times. Nero was a big culprit, mixing gold with other alloys to stretch the monetary system to pay for his lifestyle, finance the army and support the Roman bureaucracy. This practice, in addition to "clipping"— shaving gold from coin edges to produce more coins— was one of history's first lessons in inflation.

With some bumps along the way, the coinage system of commerce worked well for hundreds if not 1,000 years. But as trade grew around the world in volume and value, it became apparent that some form of paper money had to be introduced. The Chinese had figured out paper money as early as 800 during the reign of Hien Tsung. Years later, Marco Polo would describe the paper money used by Kublai Khan as "magic." The paper was actually mulberry tree bark cut into various sizes to represent different denominations, then stamped with the seal of the Great Khan. Under his orders, every payment in the kingdom had to be made using the paper money. Unfortunately for Kublai Khan, the only place the paper had value was within his empire.[4] But by the Middle Ages, the notion of using paper money had forced itself onto the doorsteps of most European countries. Great Britain, being the financial powerhouse of the day, took the greatest strides towards instituting paper money with the distribution of Bank of England banknotes.[5] The notes were redeemable for a set amount of gold. The specified amount was arrived at by Newton in 1717, which brings us back to the first date on Marotta's chart, because this was the advent of the gold standard. Newton fixed the price at £3, 17 shillings and 10 pence per troy ounce. The ability to exchange notes for gold was called convertibility.

Because the gold standard obligated the Bank of England to have the same amount of gold on hand as the amount of money in circulation, it forced a fiscal responsibility on the government to print only as much money as they had gold to support it. This became problematic for a number of reasons. Supporting costly wars and paying troops to fight in them were among the biggest draws on government coffers. During the Napoleonic Wars, Britain quickly found itself short of gold to support its spending desires. Hence, convertibility was suspended and the government printed more money between 1797 and 1821. Convertibility would be suspended several times over the next 150 years as various countries took on costly wars and other major expenses. After the First World War, Britain again suspended convertibility, as did the Americans during the Civil War, the Great Depression and after the Second World War. By this time, real world economics and commerce were, in fact, making the whole notion of a gold standard difficult to maintain. Governments wanting to run deficits were unable to do so without making life—particularly during the Depression—extremely difficult for voters. Rather than stimulate an economy with spending, governments of the day had to rein it in to ensure they had enough gold to cover their debts. Taxes were also often raised during these times to raise money for more gold purchases, which only made life tougher. With regard to trade, the idea of ferrying gold in ships from one country to another was also getting silly. Yes, that's actually how they used to transfer wealth.

Although everyone agreed the system needed fixing, no one wanted to let go of the gold standard. In an attempt to improve things, 44 countries gathered in the New Hampshire resort of Bretton Woods in 1944 to make plans for a new international economic order.[6] The centrepiece of the new arrangement provided that the U.S. would be the only nation with a currency freely convertible into gold at a fixed rate. Other countries were obligated to ensure their currencies could be converted into the U.S. dollar, but did not have to maintain convertibility into gold. The U.S. did, as a result, become the reserve currency, and, as Marotta's chart showed, the price of gold was pegged at US$35 an ounce after the meeting.

Again, it was a war and a tough economy that ate away at the foundations of this arrangement. The Vietnam War was expensive, the U.S. found it difficult to match other countries' demands for gold and the economy of the day was deteriorating, and this continued for several years. President Richard Nixon responded in 1971 by closing the so-called "gold window"—the U.S. government would no longer offer any convertibility from paper to gold. This marked the end of the gold standard and the introduction of fiat money. *Fiat* simply means *decree*: with the introduction of fiat money, governments decree that all people accept paper as legal tender without any gold backing the currency. The end of convertibility has many implications in our story today. The first of these implications was a free-floating gold price, which is why the price of gold as it appears on the chart begins to fluctuate after 1971. The surge in gold at the end of that decade is also apparent, as is the bust that followed. By 1997, the average price of gold over the year was US$331.02 an ounce compared to an average of US$615 in 1980.

The downward pressure on the price of gold in 1997 was coming from a variety of sources. The first downward pressure was the growing perception that gold was no longer a store of value. With the gold standard a distant memory, central bankers were left scratching their heads as to why they held so much of this metal that no longer backed a currency. Gold had become, to many central bankers, a curiosity no longer needed as a monetary asset or for price stability. Secondary downward pressures came as a result of this change in perception: the bankers now valued gold differently. Ten years earlier, only half of central bankers priced their gold reserves at market value, but by 1997, two-thirds of central bankers let the market determine the value. Central banks wanted a better return on their money and interest-yielding assets in the form of government bonds were calling.

Adding to the pressure was a June 1997 discussion paper issued by the Fed suggesting that central banks would be better off selling their gold reserves. Gold held in vaults, the report proposed, was a wasted asset. If all countries sold their gold, the authors concluded, it would over time amount to a net gain in value to the holders of US$368 billion. The thought was not new, but the fact that it came on the Fed's letterhead made it news. When the group that holds 25% of global gold reserves starts asking whether gold could be put to better use, it makes headlines.[7]

If the love affair with gold was over among central bankers, it was worse among investors. Between 1987 and 1997, gold was the worst-performing asset class. If you invested US$100 in the S&P 500 stock index in 1987, you would've netted $350 by 1997, whereas you'd have $70 in your pocket if you made that same $100 investment in gold.[8] In Canada, the Bre-X story was about to dash the hopes of even the most diehard gold bugs. I remember distinctly that, at its peak, Bre-X was about the fifteenth-largest company in the Canadian index. So, percentage-wise, Bre-X was as big in Canada as Gillette was in the United States. The company, which had begun trading on the Alberta stock exchange in May 1988 at 30 cents a share, had a net market worth over $6 billion on the TSX in early 1998. By 1998 it was trading for $280 dollars a share. The company's most recent upgrade—one in a series—pegged the number of ounces of retrievable gold at 200 million ounces, up from the 39-million-ounce estimate posted a couple of years earlier.[9] The house of cards, as we know, fell shortly thereafter, adding cynicism to investors' distaste for gold.

Another sign of the times came from well-known miner and Canadian financier Pierre Lassonde. He is chairman of royalty company Franco-Nevada, former President of Newmont Mining Corp. and past chairman of the World Gold Council so he and his circle of friends know a thing or two about gold. When Lassonde came to visit investors in Boston in 1999, he told us he had surveyed gold companies, and the overwhelming majority thought the price of gold was never going up. This was the view *inside* the industry. By just about every measure—valuation, sentiment and fundamentals—you should have dismissed gold from your mind, and a lot of investment management firms dropped their gold industry coverage because the sector was held in such disrepute. But Team Canada didn't, and we had the perfect opportunity because the veteran who had grown leery of Bre-X had decided to move on to another role at Fidelity. So we had a vacancy, one that we filled with Marotta, which brings us back to that lunch presentation.

After taking the group through gold's price history, industry fundamentals and the companies he thought would perform best out of a bad lot in 1999, Marotta concluded with the news of the day. In May, the U.K. central bank announced it would start disposing of 395 tons of gold, or more than half its gold reserve. That turned out to be 395 tonnes, which was sold in 20- and 25-tonne lots every two months starting July 1999.* They sold about half shortly thereafter, with the remainder earmarked for disposal over the coming months. When the stack of gold—almost as big as two London taxis— was finally sold, the highest price they got for it was US$296.50 an ounce, not much above the 20-year low. And that was it for half their reserves. Gone. Sold at the bottom. The U.K. collected gold through thousands of years of conquest, then one day, they decide to sell half the reserves at rock-bottom prices. That's just perfect. Years after, the British public continues to seethe. The *Sunday Times* still sarcastically refers to the chancellor

---

*In the English or U.S. system, the *ton* is sometimes referred to as the *short ton* or *net ton*. It is equal to 2,000 pounds. The *long ton*, sometimes referred to as the *gross ton*, on the other hand, is equal to 2,240 pounds. When reading the word *ton*, one should always assume the short ton (2,000 pounds), unless stated otherwise. In the metric system, the *metric ton* is equal to 1,000 kilograms (2,205 pounds) and is frequently spelled *tonne*, to distinguish it from the *ton*.

who initiated the sale, Gordon Brown, as "Goldfinger Brown." Gold traders refer to the period as the "Brown Bottom."

The U.K move came swift on the heels of the Swiss dropping their gold standard in April 1999. Switzerland had been on the gold standard for over a century. And just like that, they decide to break the link between the country's gold reserves and the amount of currency in circulation. Sales of "surplus" gold—1,300 tonnes, or around half the total reserve—commenced five months later in September 1999. Come December, the Netherlands announced its intention to sell 300 tonnes.* Meanwhile, Canada had been busy selling what would amount to more than 400 tonnes starting in 1990.[10] Add to that the 12 tonnes Germany sold in 2000, and I thought to myself, "It's amazing all these countries would do this after 20 years of decline."

The only explanation I could muster is that it was bureaucrats like Brown who were doing the selling. The old countries of Switzerland and the U.K. have held gold since 1500 or 1600—I mean, the *year* 1600—and they chose this moment in time to part with it, their accumulated wealth of the ages. The kings we read about in Shakespeare risked and lost their lives for this gold, and then one day this bureaucrat comes along and sells

---

*To see a list of central bank gold sales from 1999–2009, the World Gold Council has a good list with explanatory notes: http://www.gold.org/deliver.php?file=/value/stats/statistics/xls/CBGA_sales_current.xls.

it at a terribly low price. I'm going to guess it was some quick accounting fix he was looking for to meet some silly budget deficit or to pay off some new government program. If you think about it, if you put it in the context of what the country had to do to get this gold, the Brown Bottom and the rest of the gold fire sale marked the start of a decline for the West. The fact that they were selling it was indicative not only of the bottom price of gold but also of a changing world order. By selling off their gold, they were validating the end of the gold standard and also asserting that printing paper money is equal to or better than holding real assets. They were also validating a point that keeps coming up. The U.S., U.K., Europe and Japan continue to sell assets and print money to maintain social entitlements. Meanwhile, the buyers of these scarce resources are the ones now creating wealth through savings, investment and production.

The gold companies had also started hedging their gold—selling future production at pre-set prices— because they were convinced it wasn't going anywhere but down. I'm not sure if I made the comment, or if someone else at the table did, but it went along these lines: "We can never figure out exactly when we hit bottom, but this sure feels like the bottom."

I could tell Marotta, who subsequently went on to be an executive at a Canadian gold mining company, had hit a home run. The best way to judge the success of an industry review is by the number of questions after, and there were plenty after Marotta's presentation, particularly from the U.S. equity side as portfolio managers in Canada are more in step with gold. I got up and went over to the whiteboard and invited Marotta and the rest of the folks in the room to write down their predictions for the price of gold. The first came in at $400, the second $450 and a third at $600. I scrawled $1,000 on the board and everyone smiled.

"It couldn't happen," someone remarked.

Although gold is found everywhere on the planet, no place has yielded as much as South Africa. A relative newcomer to the scene, South Africa has stocked the vaults, fed the mints and adorned people's heads, ears and fingers with more gold than any other country since that fateful day in 1886 when George Harrison happened on an outcrop of gold while digging up stone to build a house.[11]

Ironically, the find was originally considered a dud. The geology below the Witwatesrand Basin in South Africa where Harrison was digging is such that gold runs in large blankets—or reefs—deep below the surface. These reefs are on average about a foot thick and the gold is contained in bodies of ore that don't make for easy pickings. In fact, a ton of rock holds but one ounce of gold and, much to the disappointment of the miners, the gold does not easily dislodge from the rock.[12]

The South African situation stood in stark contrast to

what was required to mine for gold during the California gold rush of 1849. In 1848, John Sutter contracted a builder to erect a saw mill near the Sacramento River in California. Sutter's builder found gold, the two men became partners and the rest is history as thousands of people invaded the area by 1849.[13] The method employed by the gold seekers was simple enough. Gold, which had been entombed in the rock of the surrounding hills and mountains, had been slowly lifted from it over millions of years due to weather erosion. The fine grains of gold were washed into fast-moving streams and rivers below where it was carried by the current to spots where the water widened or slowed, allowing the dense gold to sink to the bottom and mix with sand and gravel. Using pans with filters—a lesson taken from the ancient Greeks who used sheepskins in the same manner as pans, hence the myth of the Golden Fleece—the sand and gravel would travel through the filter leaving the gold behind.[14]

In South Africa, on the other hand, the miners who rushed to Harrison's property unearthed and piled high huge mountains of rock, but had very little gold to show for it. Worse, as people dug deeper, the gold seemed to run thinner. Within two years, Harrison sold his property for 10 pounds, the stocks of several mining companies crashed and the story appeared to be over, a recurring theme when it comes to investing in gold. In 1889, however, a man by the name of Allan James made the trip to South Africa claiming he and his company could extract the gold from the rock using a chemical process called cyanidation. James was right and the impact was immediate. Gold production rose from less than a ton in 1886 to over 120 tons by 1889.[15]

Although it has been improved and mechanized over the years, the cyanidation process remains fairly unchanged today. The mountain of rock that comes from the mines is crushed and then treated with a variety of chemicals, the most active of which is arsenic. The chemicals interact with the various compounds in the rock, ultimately loosening the gold, which is then collected and treated again before it heads off for further processing. Most people would be surprised to discover how little gold you actually see at these mines. When I was in Klipfontein, South Africa in 1992 I visited a mine as part of a fact-finding mission. All I saw was a bunch of rock, dirt and earth. There were no gold bars or nuggets coming out of the ground. In fact, it's very much an industrial process and not nearly as glamorous as it might seem. While I was there, I visited the mine head and ventured down a shaft a couple of hundred feet. I was invited to go further, but I'm a bit claustrophobic and the thought of going thousands of feet underground was something I chose not to do. Mine was a luxury not afforded by the millions of South African miners who have risked and a good many lost their lives toiling in 50 degree Celsius temperatures in damp, dark, cramped places miles beneath the earth.

Thanks to their efforts, South Africa has been the source of close to 40% of all the gold ever produced. The banner year came in 1970 when the country produced over 65% of the world's production with more than 32 million ounces pulled from the ground. It's been downhill ever since. With the passage of each successive year, South Africa's production has slipped. By 2000, the country's share of world production had dropped to 16% and the total gold it extracted stood at 13.8 million ounces.[16]

Raising the microscope higher, another trend was developing in gold production by 2000. Although other countries had picked up the slack from South Africa, it wasn't enough to make up the shortfall. As a result, global gold production has been in a steady decline since it peaked in 2000. That's when the earth yielded 2,700 tons of gold. In 2009, that figure was down to 2,300 tons.[17]

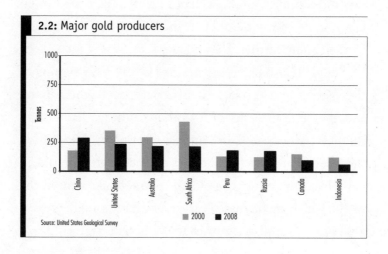

2.2: Major gold producers

Tonnes

Source: United States Geological Survey

■ 2000 ■ 2008

China, United States, Australia, South Africa, Peru, Russia, Canada, Indonesia

Historically, declining production has moved in near lockstep with falling gold prices. The fact that we have some of the highest dollar figures in front of gold yet declining production tells you something. There are no more easy pickings with gold. That's one of the reasons I think gold will boom. The metal has always been scarce, but new supply has always come on stream, particularly when prices were high. Remember the late 1970s and early 1980s? That was the last time we saw a spike in the gold price, and over the course of the next five to 10 years we saw production ramped up as capital found its way into the industry and the sector expanded. This is not the case today. Gold is over US$1,000 an ounce yet production is down even though companies are going to greater lengths to find it. The Mponeng mine, owned by AngloGold Ashanti, is going deeper than any other mine in the world to depths of 11,350 feet.[18] That's more than two miles underground, a depth greater than the Grand Canyon. And AngloGold isn't the only company reaching further, going farther. They all are.

Supply is also being constrained by the 1999 signing of the Washington Agreement. The European Central Bank and the central banks of 14 other countries had set up camp as part of the IMF's annual meeting in Washington that year. One of the main topics of discussion was gold, in particular, the selling of gold by central banks around the world, which we discussed earlier. The bank sales depressed gold prices, and for countries that still had large holdings, the drop in price was making them squirmy. In an effort to protect the value of current bank reserves, the central bank governors drafted the Washington Agreement to curtail sales for the next five years. The agreement has subsequently been extended twice through 2014.[19]

Central banks have operated as virtual gold mines for years by selling their supplies on the open market. By agreeing to discontinue sales, they put another squeeze on supply. Further, the signatories to this agreement agreed not to expand their gold leasings and their use of gold futures and options over this period. Throughout the 1990s, many central banks leased gold to bullion banks to prop up their currencies. This further suppressed gold prices, as the banks did not have to buy gold on the open market when the leases expired. By curtailing gold leasing, central banks will have to go to market instead of leasing, which should have the effect of increasing spot prices. The use of futures and options (derivative investment instruments based on the underlying current and future price of gold) had also been nixed, thereby lifting another drag on gold.

Meanwhile, on the demand side, there was another interesting development starting around 2000. The developing countries of the world started buying gold. China has increased reserves of the metal by 76% to about 1,000 tonnes since 2003. In 2004, Argentina bought about 50 tonnes and in October 2009 India scooped up 200 tonnes—the single biggest central bank purchase in 30 years. Russia, meantime, has taken its gold reserves

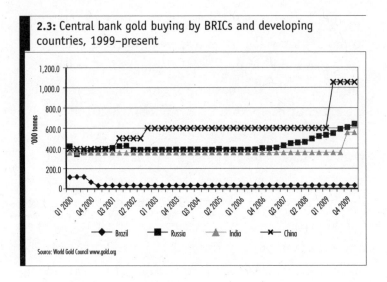

2.3: Central bank gold buying by BRICs and developing countries, 1999–present

Source: World Gold Council www.gold.org

from 422 tonnes to 663 tonnes from the first-quarter 2000 to the first-quarter 2010.[20]

A couple of factors motivate these purchases by developing countries. The first and most important is that developing countries now have the wherewithal to finance the buying. Due to industrialization, they are growing, making things, exporting them and acquiring foreign reserves in the process. And just as any investor would want to diversify and prepare for a rainy day, countries— or more specifically, their central bankers—want to have gold as part of their reserves, which are currently stuffed with U.S. dollars. Unlike the paper money, the value of which is based on trust, gold is a hard asset and it has outlived every currency ever invented.

China, which up until early 2010 had the highest

exposure to the U.S. dollar, has stated publicly that it is concerned about the lack of diversification in its reserves and is doing something about it. Other developing countries are doing likewise and I think they'll keep buying until their gold reserves rise to percentage levels equivalent to the developed world. And they have a long way to go. On average, the Indias, Chinas and Russias of the world have less than 5% of their foreign reserves allocated to gold, whereas the developed world has about twice that, over 10%.[21]

In terms of preparing for a rainy day, many developing countries remember the bruising their currencies have experienced from time to time. Whether it was Mexico in 1994, the Asian currency crisis of 1997 or Russia in the same decade, many countries have lived through the painful consequences of large devaluations in their currencies. Gold is one way to fight runs on a currency as it can be used as an asset to buy and increase the value of a home country's money.

Preparing for a rainy day and diversifying foreign reserves are only part of the story. There has also been a noticeable swing back to the notion that fiat money may not be so great after all. That may be the biggest driver behind gold demand. It's only been 40-odd years since we went off the gold standard and already some wrinkles are starting to appear. The big one is the concern that the guys printing the money may not be able to pay it back. Due to the huge increase in money supplies by many developed

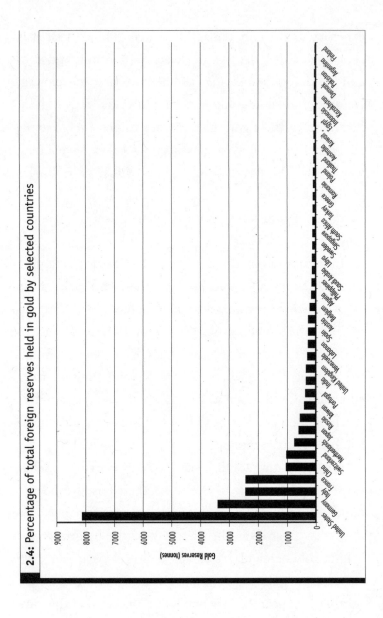

2.4: Percentage of total foreign reserves held in gold by selected countries

countries—the U.S., Britain, Germany, France—the BRICs and others are wondering whether money is really worth the paper it's printed on. The Greek debt crisis and ensuing European Union bailout has underscored the growing nervousness about paper money. The credit rating agency Moody's has said the U.S. could lose its top rating if it doesn't reduce its deficit to a sustainable level in the next couple of years. That heightens the uncertainty even in light of the pledge by the G20 countries in Toronto to rein in their spending, halve their deficits by 2013 and stabilize their debt three years later. These are verbal commitments made by politicians who understand the direction of political winds. But as the months pass and the voting populations in Europe contemplate a future with fewer entitlements, longer working lives and smaller pension cheques, the pledges made in Toronto could easily recede into history.

What if, for instance, the world goes back to a gold standard to counter reckless fiscal, monetary and trade policies? Gold is a very tiny fraction of the global money supply and financial assets around the world.

A very tiny supply. At last count, there's about US$5 trillion worth of gold versus a global money supply of over US$60 trillion and US$200 trillion in financial assets.

If the discussion turns to gold returning to its historic role as a currency, there is just way too little when you compare it to the amount of paper money. If that happens, the dam will break and you're going to get big t of gold prices. And if it doesn't? I think

g to see big numbers, just not as big. That's

y always takes a back seat during a boom.

rs is perception; and if the perception says we need go to backstop paper currency, the upside is just beyond belief. On that basis, gold goes up to US$5,000 or US$6,000 an ounce or something crazy like that.

Gold's upside price potential also ties to money printing, which has occurred since 2008 and has the world talking about inflation. As the monetary base expands, so does money supply, and as it grows, so does inflation. It's a three-stepper in terms of events: monetary base gets pumped up, money supply increases lead to inflation and inflation leads to higher gold prices, because gold has always been a good hedge against inflation.

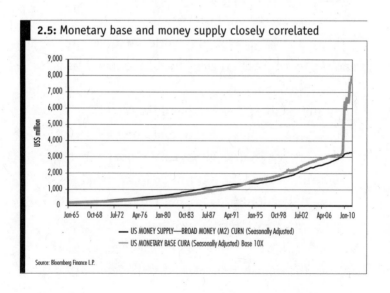

2.5: Monetary base and money supply closely correlated

— US MONEY SUPPLY—BROAD MONEY (M2) CURN (Seasonally Adjusted)
— US MONETARY BASE CURA (Seasonally Adjusted) Base 10X

Source: Bloomberg Finance L.P.

Another strong indicator of gold's potential comes in the form of a 100-year chart that plots gold against the Dow. This is one of those charts you look at only once in a blue moon. It measures pieces of paper, which we'll call stock certificates, against things that go bump in the night, which we'll call gold. The chart gives you three signals in the 100 years shown: when the line reaches the top range, the chart is saying that pieces of paper are very highly valued against things that go bump in the night. So if you look at three dates: 1929, 1969 and 2000. In all three stock certificates ruled. No one wanted the stuff that went bump in the night, or gold.

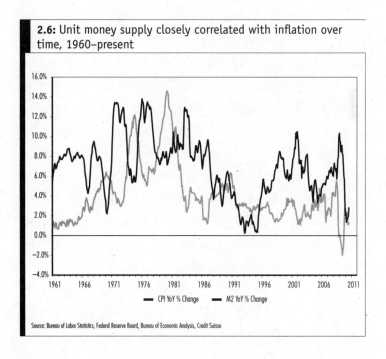

2.6: Unit money supply closely correlated with inflation over time, 1960–present

Source: Bureau of Labor Statistics, Federal Reserve Board, Bureau of Economic Analysis, Credit Suisse

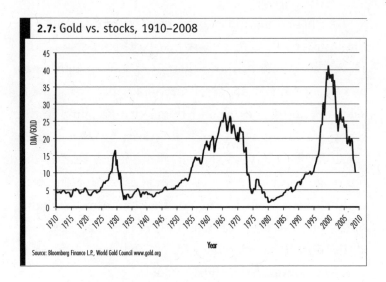

2.7: Gold vs. stocks, 1910–2008

Source: Bloomberg Finance L.P., World Gold Council www.gold.org

Now look at the bottom range in 1907, the 1930s and early 1980s: nobody wanted pieces of paper. They just wanted things that go bump in the night. Remember I told you about Morgan and Rockefeller wanting to socialize risk through the Fed's creation? That stemmed from the panic of 1907 when Morgan coordinated a personal and governmental effort to save the system. So in 1907, it was time to start buying. And the graph shows that. When gold peaked at US$810 an ounce in 1981 and the Dow was at 800 points, the situation was reversed. Everyone had sold their paper and held gold. Paper was never cheaper. It was time to buy stocks.

So if gold goes to a multiple of two and the Dow does nothing, gold's US$5,000 an ounce. Could the Dow go down and gold up to US$3,000. Who knows?

Bringing us to modern day, we see the value of things that go bump in the night is about one-tenth that of pieces of paper. Gold is essentially in the middle range with the Dow 10 times the price of gold. This tells me that gold has plenty of room to move up, and for the average Joe, I can't think of a better, simpler indicator.

So what's the impact on the S&P/TSX? Gold stocks represent a meaningful slice of the overall index, which means a move in the gold price is a key accelerator for many companies listed on the Toronto Stock Exchange. A closer look reveals something more interesting. That composition makes the TSX number one in the world in terms of investable gold stocks. *Investable* meaning they are liquid, regulated and trustworthy. The MSCI AC World Index Gold industry subgroup values of investable gold stocks in Canada at almost $100 billion. South Africa is second at $21.5 billion, the U.S. third at $20.8 billion and Australia fourth at $13 billion. You can forget about Russia and China. Yes, they do have a small market weight in gold stocks, but if I have to choose between a Canadian-domiciled gold company and one that's headquartered in Russia, I'll go with Canada. And I think the rest of the world feels the same way. Whether you're an individual investor or an investment or hedge fund manager, the world's going to come shopping for Canadian gold companies.

It won't be just the big producers that people will invest in. A wide range of other large-, mid- and

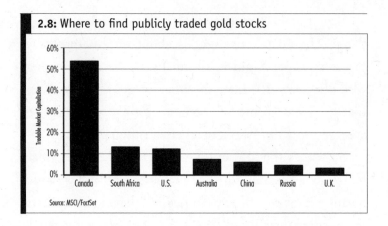

2.8: Where to find publicly traded gold stocks

Source: MSCI/FactSet

small-cap companies are also poised to benefit, as are a raft of tertiary firms that supply equipment, technology and know-how to the industry. There are also companies such as Franco-Nevada, a royalty company, which is another way to invest in gold. Regardless of the strategy you employ, this is gold's time to shine.

When you think about it, is it so strange that after thousands of years, we're still obsessing over gold, its new finds and booms? I think not. Since the beginning of time, gold has been universally recognized as a store of value and I can't see any reason why that would change in our age. Long after this boom is over, a long cycle of bust is sure to follow because I believe we will find more gold over the next 10 to 15 years or we will develop a new way to get at some of the stuff that currently eludes us. But that isn't going to happen anytime soon. That's why gold deserves its place as a leading player in the boom. Now it's time to see why oil warrants the same consideration.

CHAPTER THREE

Oil

"Canada is an emerging energy superpower"
CANADIAN PRIME MINISTER STEPHEN HARPER, JULY 2006

The annual Goldman Sachs Global Energy Conference is a rite of passage for anyone involved in the energy business: company executives from the major oil and gas producers, suppliers, drillers, explorers, sell-side investors, investment banking chiefs, portfolio managers, analysts and of course, buy-side investors such as us.

More important, it's a rite of passage for any analyst who's new to the sector. Not because the information is great; it isn't. And not because the insights are good; they're not. No, what's important is the *feel* of the place. Based on conference attendance, the amount of wine consumed by attendees, the food served and the mood of the people, you can learn a lot about the state of the industry. That impression becomes one more piece of the investment mosaic you build as you think about a company or an industry. Sometimes the mosaic builds quickly and you're able to get a clear read. Other times—and this is usually the case—it builds slowly, each piece falling into place over months, sometimes years.

When oil is going gangbusters there's real excitement at the conference. You can feel the enthusiasm. It's exciting. I made my first pilgrimage in 1986 and try to attend every second or third year. The particular conference I have in mind was in 2000 and this year's edition was being held at New York's Waldorf Astoria Hotel. I brought Team Canada's newest member and energy analyst with me.

In my role as U.S. research director and Canadian CIO, I hired scores of analysts over the years. In addition to the normal interview process, I instituted what's called the "ticker test." The test was simple enough. I gave the candidate a stock symbol and two weeks to research a company. At the end of two weeks, he or she would appear before a panel of portfolio managers and present his or her case to invest or not invest in the company. In the case of the energy analyst with me at the conference, I gave him the symbol CVE. The symbol stood for sneaker-maker Converse. What most candidates did—after they looked up the stock symbol—was pour over annual reports, take apart balance sheets, review earnings statements, dig into publicly available analysts reports and so on.

And this was the case with this particular analyst. But in addition to doing the expected, he also went to inner city playgrounds in Boston where kids were playing basketball. He interviewed as many as he could, asking them what they thought of the new Converse line and whether they would buy them or not. He spent a week doing this. One week out of the two he had to complete the assignment.

On the day of the presentation he finished by saying, "Bob, do not buy Converse. They are not resonating with the key target audience—kids in the street. This will not play out well in the long term."

The actions the analyst took were unique. He stood out. We didn't pay him to do this. We didn't tell him what to do. We gave him a ticker symbol, a company he'd never researched, and he figured the rest out.

He got the job. And Converse went bankrupt.

At the conference in New York, we listened to about a half dozen presentations and talked to industry participants and investors from both the buy and sell sides. Overall, the mood was terrible. Oil and anything energy had been in the dumpster for the better part of 20 years. Production was being ratcheted down around the world, new projects were on hold and no new money was flowing into the oil sector. Layoffs at the majors had become commonplace and the juniors were finding it difficult to get any financing.

On the flight home, I asked the analyst what he thought of the conference.

"I thought it was pretty good," he said without having past years' conferences to put the most recent one in context.

I kept quiet. I could tell no one was happy. Even the bartenders looked morose. When we reached cruising altitude, I looked out the window and saw New York fading in the distance and the rest of the Eastern seaboard stretching out before us. I thought of the houses, the cars and the buildings as the sound of the jets levelled off to become a whiny hum. I thought to myself how none of this could keep moving without oil behind it. And with the industry in the dumps, I couldn't help thinking what would spur the next big up cycle in oil. I had no doubt it would happen. Oil is the biggest commodity in the world, and the minute it stops commanding attention is usually the time to start paying attention.

When I arrived at the office the next morning, the first thing I did was prepare to boost our energy analyst coverage. Up until then, we had the one analyst responsible for the majors, independents and services. He was spread too thin. And the opportunity, in my mind, was too great to pass up. I liked what I saw at the conference. There was real negative sentiment surrounding the whole industry. I knew it couldn't last, but just wasn't sure what the trigger would be.

The big fear with oil is running out of it. That's what's driven every boom in oil and it's what will drive it in the coming years.

The first time we experienced this fear, or "oil shock" as it has been dubbed by the media, it crept into our hearts during the Arab-Israeli conflict of 1973. That's when a number of Arab countries and Iran turned off the taps and stopped exporting crude to the U.S. The Arab oil embargo stemmed from U.S. support for Israel during the Yom Kippur War. The images of long lineups at the pumps, jerry cans in the hands of men wearing suits and the accompanying sky-high oil prices had people fearful that maybe, just maybe we might run out of crude. The episode turned out to be short-lived as diplomacy brought an end to the embargo by March 1974. The second oil shock occurred in 1979 and spilled into the early 1980s. It was sparked first by the Iranian revolution. Iran, which had supplied the world with 2 to 2.5 million barrels of oil a day, almost completely halted production for eight months. The revolution preceded the invasion of Iran by Iraq in 1980, which curtailed production again. The combination of the two events led to the highest price for oil in since the Second World War.[1]

The impact of the oil shocks was twofold. On the one hand, it led to a massive conservation effort in most oil-consuming countries, particularly the United States. Millions of homes were properly insulated for the first time, cars were mandated to meet new efficiency standards and the development of alternate sources of energy, namely nuclear power, came to the fore. The second impact was massive new exploration efforts across the globe to find new sources of oil. This was the period when new supplies were found in the North Sea off Great Britain, in Alaska, Mexico and Canada, where the large Leduc fields were opened in Alberta in the mid-1970s, eventually leading to the oil sands discovery.

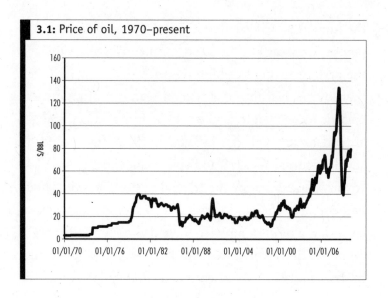

3.1: Price of oil, 1970–present

Throughout the rest of the 1980s and 1990s, the fear of running out was pushed to the sidelines. There was relative calm in the world politically, new vibrant sources of oil had come on stream and the price of oil reflected the sense of security with prices falling from their 1980s highs. The relative calm led to a false sense of security and the amount of capital expenditures flowing into oil slowed to a trickle, as if there would never be another up cycle.

At the same time, dramatic changes were occurring in distant corners of the world. The rise of developing countries' economies had begun. China caught my attention first. Not because it was a new story but because it was a potentially big story. Most everyone was aware of China's decision to come off pure communism, but not

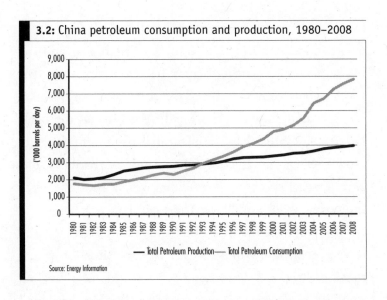

3.2: China petroleum consumption and production, 1980–2008

— Total Petroleum Production ---- Total Petroleum Consumption

Source: Energy Information

everyone connected the dots between industrialization, billions of people and oil consumption. This blind spot wasn't surprising. An announcement of change is not the same as actual change. And China, even with its massive population, was such a small consumer and maker of things that few gave it much thought. Plus, it was a story that was quiet in the making unless you had an eye for it. In 1985, for example, China consumed about 2 million barrels of crude a day while producing about 2.5 million barrels, so it was actually a very small net exporter, but it's irrelevant on a world scale. Start to roll the clock forward and by 2000, China is consuming 4 million barrels a day. So it takes 15 years to double and by 2000, they're now a net importer of crude to the tune of roughly a million or a million and a half barrels a day. Now we're getting into some serious numbers. You roll the clock forward again and China has really gone into high gear and the big numbers are getting bigger. It's about this time that the numbers started to make the front pages of business sections as opposed to the small news bites at the back. By 2008, China has doubled its consumption again. Now the country is consuming 8 million barrels a day and producing about 4 million, which means they're importing about 4 million barrels per day.

This represented new demand as opposed to the replacement of anything. So you've got a situation where the industrialized countries of the world have reached stability in terms of oil consumption. The big developed countries, such as the U.S., Japan and all of Europe, have reached their highest points of oil use. The U.S. consumes roughly one in every four barrels of oil produced every day, or 19.4 million barrels out of a world total of 84.4 million.[2] Those figures come from 2008, but they're the same numbers you saw in 2007, 2000 and so on. So the U.S. is stuck, as are most developed countries. You get to a certain level of oil consumption and then you stay there.

The correlation between GDP growth and oil consumption is well understood and follows a pre-set path. Oil use is at the heart of most industrial activity. As countries industrialize, the demand for oil spikes as they build stuff, run iron, steel and machinery plants and manufacture goods, using oil both as an input (petrochemicals) and as fuel. As GDP grows, per capita incomes begin to rise. In other words, standards of living improve and people begin to purchase such things as cars. Transportation is the single biggest user of oil in the world, as illustrated by the 61.4% of annual consumption

Bubbling crude: the one-two oil punch

Rarely in human history have we seen such a large increase in oil demand. On the one hand, you've got the rising consumer impact (per capita oil consumption) from nearly half the world's population, who will be pumping more to fuel new cars and heat homes as they climb the economic development ladder. And on the other, you've got growing populations and rising industrial needs, which will further boost consumption leading to an oil super-cycle.

3.3: The conceptual global S-curve—per capita oil consumption

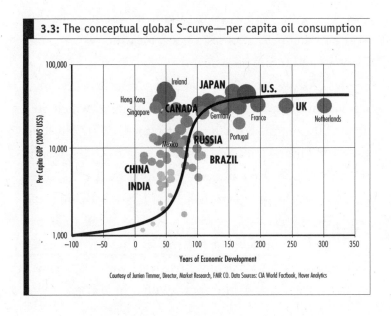

Courtesy of Jurrien Timmer, Director, Market Research, FMR CO. Data Sources: CIA World Factbook, Hoover Analytics

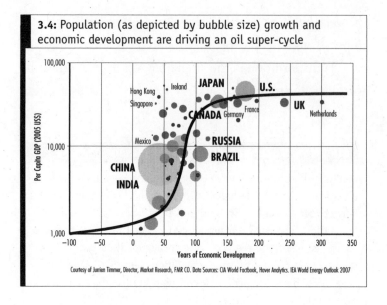

3.4: Population (as depicted by bubble size) growth and economic development are driving an oil super-cycle

Courtesy of Jurrien Timmer, Director, Market Research, FMR CO. Data Sources: CIA World Factbook, Haver Analytics. IEA World Energy Outlook 2007

which the U.S. pumped into gas tanks in 2008 (the figure was 45.3% in 1973).[3] As a result, the number of cars sold in a country becomes a good measure of per capita incomes and future oil demand.

In 2002, China had passenger vehicle sales of 2 million in comparison to the United States, which sold about 20 million. It's a huge difference, right? In 2008, they're both at 11 million roughly. And by 2009, for the first time, more cars are sold in China than the United States. Twenty years ago, you could go to Beijing and see very few cars. Now you can't drive more than five miles an hour because of the traffic. This was predicted long ago, so China reaching that level wasn't a surprise. What *is* surprising is the speed with which it got there.

The most optimistic growth targets from analysts had the Chinese buying more cars than Americans in 2018 or 2020, somewhere in there. So the current growth rate has blown past the estimates. The total stock of cars in the world is about 800 million. That's expected to grow to over 1.3 billion by 2030, with three-quarters of the increase coming from developing countries. In fact, car ownership per capita in developing countries is expected to almost triple from 31 cars per 1,000 people in 2007 to 87 per 1,000 by 2030.[4]

That's because people from across Asia and South America love their wheels as much as we do. The question of ownership comes down to affordability. With incomes rising, cars are becoming affordable as illustrated by the 1,000 new cars that roll onto China's streets every day. In terms of car penetration rates, the numbers across developing countries have a long way to go before they catch up to the U.S. and Japan. According to UBS, 4% of Chinese over the age of 14 and 1% of Indians own cars. In the States, it's 44%, and in Japan, 46%. If car penetration rates in China and India were to rise to American and Japanese levels, you can imagine the impact that would have on oil consumption. Remember, transportation is the biggest consumer of oil, and as much as we might like to think electric cars are around the corner, you can bet the 1,000 cars a day that are currently hitting the streets in China run on gas or diesel.

Meantime, the Chinese oil consumption story is

being repeated—albeit to a lesser extent—in the other BRICs and a handful of other countries that have made the choice to industrialize. According to OPEC's 2009 World Oil Outlook, oil consumption in developing countries will rise by 23 million barrels a day over the 2008 to 2030 period to reach an average of 56 million barrels a day.[5] Remember, total demand today is about 85 million barrels, so you're basically adding 60% more oil customers.

In addition to industrialization, another force is at work driving long-term oil demand. It lies in population growth. World population is expected to grow by 50% by 2050 with almost the entirety of it coming from the developing world.[6] Although birth rates have been and are expected to remain static in many parts of the world, countries in Africa, South America and Asia are expected to more than make up for it.

With populations growing, the largest populations industrializing and standards of living rising, demand for oil will continue to rise. That's a given. The wild card in our unfolding story lies in supply.

Historically, the world has done a good job finding new sources of oil. It was, after all, just over 150 years ago when Edwin Drake struck the first commercial oil well in Titusville, Pennsylvania in 1859. Drake had been contracted by James Townsend, a speculator who had read a report by a Yale chemistry professor suggesting that rock oil, as it was called, could be processed and used as fuel for lamps—better lighting being a need created by America's industrialization. After many hits and misses, Drake struck oil at 70 feet and in so doing, launched the oil industry.[7] The rush to find oil spread throughout the U.S. and states such as Texas and California proved to hold large reserves.

By the turn of the century, a big new demand driver entered the scene: the automobile. This led to rapid development in the industry as geologists packed their bags heading for Asia and Latin America to look for crude. They were rewarded with big finds in Mexico, Indonesia, Venezuela and Russia, with the latter two quickly joining the U.S. in the top three producers in the world.[8]

The next big exploration drive was spurred by the World Wars. In addition to the massive amounts of oil required to fuel the war effort on both sides of the conflict, a number of countries had also started industrializing. This led to a boom in giant oil field discovery. The period from the start of 1930s through to the end of the 1970s saw 333 discoveries of oil fields containing half a billion barrels or more each. Some of the headline finds were Kirkuk in Iraq (1938), Ghawar in Saudi Arabia (1948) and Cantarell in Mexico (1976).[9] This period also saw the development of the Alberta Leduc No. 1 oil field (1947), Alaskan oil and finally, developments in the North Sea.

The motivation to find new supplies comes from one truth about oil: the moment you start pumping it from the ground, the less you have of it. Unlike gold where every single ounce ever mined is in existence today, oil goes up in smoke. Remember the oil well Drake opened in 1859? It's closed, run dry and the handmade derrick Drake built out of pine is probably in a museum somewhere.

Drake's well is representative of all the old oil in the world. In the U.S., total oil production stood at 7.4 million barrels per day in 1990. By 2010, the figure stood at 5.7—about a 30% drop. Globally, the U.S.'s share of world oil production has fallen from 21% in 1971 to 8% in 2006.[10] Cantarell, Mexico's main offshore field, was producing 2.1 million barrels a day as recently as 2004. By the end of 2009, the number was down to 600,000 barrels. Further, 23 of 32 of Mexico's largest reserves are in decline. It is now estimated that the country—once the world's seventh-largest oil producer—will become a net importer by 2017.[11]

World proven crude reserves are estimated to be about 1.3 trillion barrels of which OPEC members claim to hold about 80%.[12] By OPEC's reckoning and based on their current rate of production in 2008, they estimate their reserves will last for another 85 years. That's not long. But I don't subscribe to the whole peak oil notion either. According to the peak oil thesis, there is a finite amount of oil in the world and based on current projections we will, as a planet, reach a stage where supply simply peaks with not a drip to be found anywhere. This is doomsday type stuff. I believe we will find more, as with gold, but we're going to have to continue to work at it. This has been the history of oil since Drake. Whenever the fear of running out becomes real, the price rises and it makes economic sense to find more.

That's what took us to the North Sea and Alaska. And it's what's going to happen this time around. But it won't be easy. The amount of money dedicated to the pursuit of finding oil has jumped from US$70 billion globally in 2000 to US$250 billion in 2008 with nothing noteworthy to show for it—something oil executives freely admit, which is why they continue to open their wallets. ExxonMobil will, for instance, spend upwards of US$10 billion a year for five years to find and develop new oil projects around the world. According to OPEC, in total, the required cumulative exploration and development spending by the oil industry through 2030 is estimated to be US$2.3 trillion if it's to be successful.[13] Investments of this magnitude help identify new fields such as ones in Brazil, Kazakhstan and a handful of other places, but there will be no new production by 2020 or 2015 at the earliest.

The reason exploration costs have grown so large stems from the great lengths oil companies have to go to find it. Long before it was used for fuel for cars, lamps and heating, early civilizations would soak up oil from above-ground seeps. Seneca Indians routinely obtained oil by placing animal skins and other materials on top of seeps and ponds where oily scum had collected. The tarry bitumen for which the oil sands are famous was used as caulking for canoes, and in the earliest times, as an adhesive to seal objects and treat medical conditions.[14] In the Middle East, oil seeps were common. Early exploration and drilling procedures required little more than a straw to tap into these reserves.

Those days are gone, which explains the huge capital expenditures now required to find more oil. I thought I had seen the pinnacle when, as an energy analyst, I visited the offshore rigs in the Gulf of Mexico. Drilling for oil on water was not new in those days as much of Venezuela's big finds have come from the bottom of Lake Maracaibo.[15] But a lake and an ocean are two very different things. It was 1985 or '86, I can't remember the year exactly or even which company invited me, but I took a 30-minute helicopter flight from New Orleans out to the platform. I had worked with pretty big stuff in refineries, but this was beyond that. The scale of everything from the valves to the pipes and the legs of the platform descending into the water were pretty intense. Especially when you think about the equipment that had to be hauled out there and the work that went into building the rig.

Offshore drilling came into being after the last great exploration expansion of the late 1970s and '80s. That's when the North Sea off Great Britain was developed and it laid the foundation for the next level of water exploration, which is called deepwater. Now made infamous by the 2010 Gulf oil spill following the explosion of BP's (British Petroleum) Deepwater Horizon rig. Motivated by a shortage of onshore projects, high oil prices and good long-term demand growth, deepwater projects are attracting time, attention and capital. They are also symbolic of the direction the oil business has to go: farther and further.

In 2006, deepwater oil output accounted for a tiny fraction of overall oil production. In fact, it made up just 10% of all offshore drilling. By 2015, its total share is expected to climb to 25%—still minuscule in terms of the big picture, but important in illustrating why I believe we will continue to find oil.[16] But it won't be cheap oil. In fact, the cost of bringing a barrel of oil to market from onshore activities is about US$21.54 in the U.S. Offshore and in deepwater, the cost jumps to US$73.01 a barrel.[17] And in light of the Gulf spill in the summer of 2010, it's going to become more expensive as governments mandate new safeguards and regulations to avoid a repeat of the disaster. If the current pricing environment was softer than it is now—about US$70 a barrel—I'm not sure you'd find anybody out there looking in deepwater. Imagine the challenge. Royal Dutch Shell announced in March 2010 that it had made a significant new oil discovery in the Gulf of Mexico. The find is more than 25,000 feet below the seabed in 7,217 feet of water. BP, already one of the largest producers in the Gulf of Mexico, said in 2009 that it had found a new oil field there, Tiber, after drilling 35,000 feet.[18] Imagine, *35 thousand* feet. That's like seven miles. Seven. Compared to that, the offshore rig I was on was basically shallow water. The legs of the platform actually stood on the bottom of the Gulf. But the deepwater stuff takes it to another level. There is no way these rigs can be anchored to the ocean's floor so they not only have to float, but also maintain a drill that's got to go who knows how deep once you reach the floor. And then you've got to bring the stuff up and transport it to land while making sure your structure is able to withstand waves, storms, hurricanes and all that. It's a marvel. And they're building these things to go off the coasts of Brazil, home to the Tupi field, and Nigeria, Angola and a couple of other African countries because that's where the companies say the oil is.

Between 2006 and 2010, about US$28 billion was spent on deepwater floating production systems, plus another US$40 billion on drilling and subsea well completion. That's on top of the US$14 billion you've got to spend on flow and control lines with another US$10 billion for subsea hardware.[19] These costs don't reflect the still unknown amounts that will have to be spent preventing another Deepwater Horizon disaster. Makes you long for the good old days of a blanket and a straw. But this is the world we live in today. Many of the companies investing in deepwater exploration are the majors—the Shells, the Exxons, Chevrons and Totals—and that tells you something: there are no other cheaper, more conventional ways to get oil. The big oil extractors always take the path of least resistance. If there was more opportunity on land or simply offshore, that's where they'd be directing capital expenditures.

If successful, none of this stuff is going to be in our gas tanks until 2020, 2015 at the earliest. You can say for certain that the demand outlook for oil, again on a 10- or 20-year basis, is incredibly strong while supply remains uncertain at best, a realization that finally gripped the markets between 2000 and 2008 leading to the surge in oil prices. You could call this the third oil shock, as the price of oil jumped to a record US$147 a barrel in July 2008. I think we're in store for another shock in the not-too-distant future, which may not be great news at the pumps, but will be stellar news in the markets. Particularly for Canada, where the oil sands represent the second-largest proven reserves in the world. So what dynamics are at work that will make oil a key driver for the Toronto Stock Exchange? To understand that, we must first turn to a series of events around the world during the 1960s and 1970s.

OPEC, the Organization of Petroleum Exporting Countries, was founded in Baghdad, Iraq, in 1960. The founding members were Iran, Iraq, Kuwait, Saudi Arabia and Venezuela. These countries were subsequently joined by Qatar, Indonesia, Libya, UAE, Algeria, Nigeria, Ecuador, Angola and Gabon. Some of these countries' memberships have been suspended due to misbehaviour, whatever that is, so the group consists of about 12 nations.[20] OPEC's formation has a lot to do with the boom.

But first, the background. What brought the founders members of OPEC together were two realizations. The first lay in the growing importance of oil around the globe, and second, the lack of control they had over it both in terms of profits and production. This stemmed from colonialism. Iran gives us the best example. In 1901, William Knox D'Arcy, a British-born investor who had, by coincidence, made a fortune in the Australian gold rush, was granted exclusive rights to explore and exploit oil in Iran's southern provinces. D'Arcy struck oil in 1908, just as the British navy was converting their war ships from steam to oil, so he made two fortunes. With the First World War on the horizon, Britain made the decision to purchase 51% of the Anglo-Persian Oil Company, created after D'Arcy found oil. The company drafted a contract with the government of Iran that paid it 16% of profits with Britain keeping the rest. Over the next 30 years, the one-sided contract looked worse with the passage of time and Iran grew increasingly hostile, wanting it to be rewritten. By 1950, when Saudi Arabia and the Arabian American Oil Company (or Saudi Aramco) inked a deal, it was set at a 50-50 profit-sharing arrangement. Although this arrangement would soon be torn up, it did at the time become a benchmark of sorts for oil-rich countries wanting to leverage the know-how and expertise of others to get at and extract oil. By the time the British-controlled company in Iran agreed to redraft the original contract giving Iran 50% of the profits, it was too late. By 1951, the nationalist government of Tehran approved a measure to take control over the country's natural resources and it seized the company. Over the next 30 years, the struggle over oil between Britain and Iran led to a coup, the instalment of the Shah, another coup and ultimately the rise of the Ayatollah Khomeini in 1979 and his installation as the head of government.[21]

The point of the story stems from the desire in Iran—a desire that led to the genesis of OPEC—to take ownership and control of its oil. The birth of oil nationalism has now spread to a dozen or so of the biggest oil-producing countries that have nationalized their industries, created national companies and in many places, kicked out foreign companies. That leaves the U.S., Canada and a couple of other countries in the world where governments allow people to own not only surface rights but also rights to what lies below the surface. And from that very fact, Canada is set to boom like no other nation. In addition to having the second largest proven oil reserves in the world (Saudi Arabia is number one), it has the largest proportion of investable, stable and liquid oil assets in the world.

If you're interested in taking an equity position in oil producers, I can guarantee you're going to be interested in Canadian oil. It's addition by subtraction. You can pretty easily take away the countries where you can't invest.

These are Saudi Arabia, the Emirates and Iran, which
have national oil companies. And you can't invest in
Ecuador, Mexico or Venezuela either. And although you
can get exposure to Russian and Chinese oil companies,
I'm not sure you would want to do that because they don't
yet have a system of laws in place that you can trust. They
don't have democratically elected governments and they
don't have stable legal or political institutions. So yes, you
can buy Russian oil companies, you just may not own
them tomorrow, because the government or somebody
will take them away from you. It's not going to happen in
Canada where there are real property rights. When you
eliminate the "unsavoury" or "uninvestable" oil assets of
the world, you're left with about half, roughly, in Canada.

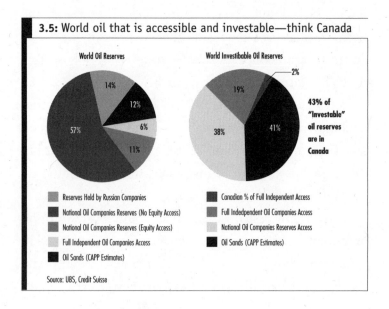

3.5: World oil that is accessible and investable—think Canada

World Oil Reserves

World Investibable Oil Reserves

43% of "Investable" oil reserves are in Canada

■ Reserves Held by Russian Companies
■ National Oil Companies Reserves (No Equity Access)
■ National Oil Companies Reserves (Equity Access)
■ Full Independent Oil Companies Access
■ Oil Sands (CAPP Estimates)

■ Canadian % of Full Independent Access
■ Full Indedpendent Oil Companies Access
■ National Oil Companies Reserves Access
■ Oil Sands (CAPP Estimates)

Source: UBS, Credit Suisse

The next logical question to ask: how much more should you be willing to pay to invest in a country or on an exchange that has a rule of law that we're all comfortable with, that has property rights and structures that we understand and believe in? You should be willing to pay a premium to invest in Canada, but Canadian oil stocks are not any more expensive than other stocks around the world. And I would argue that there are others who may want to eventually consider paying a premium, which adds impetus to the boom.

Though a premium doesn't really show in the today's Canadian markets, I think it should. I for one would pay more for an asset coming out of Alberta than I would for one out of Nigeria, all things being equal. I'll know I'll get that asset out of Alberta. Nigeria could be shut tomorrow for all I know.

That's why Canada is key when it comes to investing in the oil business. The country is never going to be the number one producer of oil, but for equity investors it should be number one when it comes to investment decisions. By investment decisions, I don't mean just stock purchases. I also mean buyouts, takeovers and mergers. That's another tailwind behind the boom that hasn't been factored into the market. Since I've worked here, I've noticed that a lot Canadians have been very willing to sell their assets at cheap prices. If you think of all the world-class companies that have disappeared in Canada, the list is long.

It suggests to me that outsiders are buying because it's cheap, they see good growth prospects and the Canadian market has been perpetually undervalued, because it's these conditions that allow for such a long list of foreign takeovers. If I told you one of the great industries emerging over the next 10 years was oil, you'd want to know how to invest in that growth. Well, the answer is Canada, and you as an investor get the infrastructure, safety and security to boot.

Strategic buyers are going to say, "Wow, we're looking around the world and we're saying we could drill off the coast of Nigeria and pay a fortune to put oil platforms and whatnot out to sea. And because it's Nigeria, we're going to expose ourselves to a lot of political risk, the threat of terrorism and a lot of other kind of infrastructural risks. Conversely, we could just go to Canada and buy the oil companies on the stock exchange and we don't have any of those risks." That's why British oil giant BP scooped up U.S. oil company Devon Energy Corporation in early 2010 for US$6 billion.[22] Although Devon is American-owned, it has both conventional and heavy oil properties in Canada, which BP likes. Tellingly, when BP decided it was time to raise cash to protect itself from takeover and possible bankruptcy following the Gulf spill, the assets it did not part with were those in the Canadian oil sands. Why? Because land has always been a safer exploration bet than water and as a result, I think you're going to see more people shopping for companies in Canada.

That to me is an investment opportunity, one that more and more people will come to see over the coming years. Canada should, as a result, be the recipient of incremental capital flows in a coming boom. The flows will enter stocks, companies and the sector as a whole. That includes suppliers, explorers, drillers and equipment makers across all market caps. You started to get a sense of that a couple of years ago in the mid-2000s when significant amounts of capital started being directed to oil.

So if you buy the fact that 10 years from now the demand for oil is going to be much higher than today with little or no new supply in sight and you're looking for a place to take advantage of that, you're going to choose to invest in Canada. At the end of the day, that's all you care about as an investor. There is no other game in town. You don't care that Saudi Arabia has tons of oil, because you can't invest in it. You're not allowed to. There's no way to get at it.

If it was coincidence that put Canada at the centre of the oil universe in terms of investing, the outcome of that fortunate placement will be anything but. The age-old fear of running out of oil will power the Toronto Stock Exchange to new heights with additional support coming from the last leading player in the boom story: agriculture.

CHAPTER FOUR

Agriculture

"The only way to make a lot of money is to go to the city."
KOU YING, FARMER, JIJIAYING, CHINA, *NEW YORK TIMES*,
APRIL 10, 1995

I n China they call it the red line. It represents the amount of cultivated land the country needs to feed itself until 2020. The red line is 120 million hectares. I don't think the Chinese have a hope of staying above it. They're already down to 122 million hectares, and arable land is shrinking fast.[1] In fact it's been cut by half in roughly a generation. In 1961, there was 0.2 hectares of arable land per person. By 2007, that figure was 0.1.[2] Put more tangibly, the country has lost the equivalent of a Sichuan, China's most populous province, in arable land. Lying atop the land are more than 500 new "officially recognized" cities. With all the good things that have come from China's industrialization, the one negative is the loss of arable land.

This situation is playing out across the world, particularly in rapidly industrializing countries. In India, the loss has been even more dramatic than in China. In 1961, the country had 0.4 hectares of arable land per person. By 2007, that was down to 0.1 hectares, having been paved over to make way for factories, cities and

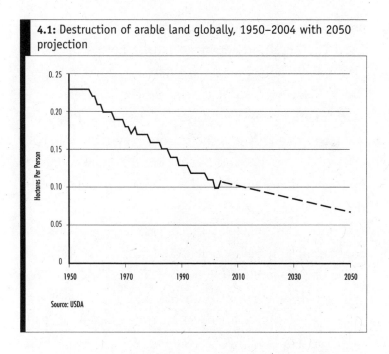

4.1: Destruction of arable land globally, 1950–2004 with 2050 projection

Hectares Per Person

0.25
0.20
0.15
0.10
0.05
0

1950   1970   1990   2010   2030   2050

Source: USDA

highways since.[3] Taking a global view, the amount of arable land per person has shrunk from 0.4 hectares per person in 1961 to 0.2 by 2007.[4]

The loss of arable land around the world is one of the factors driving the agricultural boom thesis. The others— the movement of people from farms to cities, rising standards of living and surging population growth—are impacting the world's ability to feed itself. During the next 20 years, food production may need to rise 50% to meet demand. And that would mean an additional 2.5 billion hectares of arable land would be needed at current levels. But only 700 million incremental hectares of good land exist.[5] The companies that hold some of the keys to alleviating the problem reside on the Toronto Stock Exchange, which is why agricultural deserves its place among the leading players in the boom. But before we get to the TSX and the reasons why it stands at the intersection of the world's solution for more food, let's first get a better understanding of the dynamics behind the food security issue.

Once industrialization moves into high gear, it is only a matter of time before arable land starts disappearing. If you're planning to build a city, or a factory for that matter, you're not going to put it on the side of a mountain or in some far-off place away from things such as roads, highways and ports. You're going to look for flatland that makes construction easier. You're also going to want a source of water because factories and people need plenty of water. So you tend to put them in the exact same places where you had farmland. I was talking to a friend's wife the other night at dinner and she works at a company that's building a manufacturing plant in Vietnam. I asked her, "Where is the plant going to be?" And she said, "They're building it on a rice paddy."

That makes sense. Not just from an ease-of-development perspective, but also from an economic point of view. If you've got a few hundred people toiling in a rice paddy and a company is willing to invest somewhere between $30 million and $50 million to build a plant and give 300 people jobs that pay two to three times as much as they made growing rice, it's a no-brainer. You fill in the rice paddy because you can redirect the proceeds that come from the $50-million plant to buy the rice you're no longer growing. And you can buy a hell of a lot of rice. That's what happened in Japan. For a long, long time, Japan was an agricultural country completely self-sufficient in livestock, rice, soybeans and everything. And then they made their choice and their lifestyle changed. They industrialized. Countries that were once able to feed themselves are now charging down this industrialization path and are finding it difficult to remain self-sufficient in terms of agriculture. They're going to let the rest of the world pick up the slack and use their foreign currency reserves to import beef, wheat, whatever they need. That's what Taiwan, South Korea and Japan did and China is on pace to do the same in the next five to 10 years. India is facing similar prospects.

In addition to the loss of arable land from industrial construction, land is also lost to residential development as people move from farms to cities. Globally, the percentage of people living in urban areas has jumped from 32.8% in 1960 to 49.9% in 2008. In China, those numbers look even more dramatic. In 1960, 16% of the population lived in cities compared to 43.1% in 2008. In India, the numbers are 17.6% versus 29.5% and in Brazil over 85% of people make cities their home in 2008 compared to 44.9% in 1960.[6]

The big draw for these people are jobs that pay two to three times more than a farmer would make tilling land or tending a rice paddy. Looking forward, an anticipated 2 billion people in the world will transition from rural to urban life. Residential development, like industrial construction, carries similar costs in terms of arable land loss. For every million people moving to the city, an estimated 40,000 hectares of land are required to meet non-farm uses.[7] These include everything from houses to condominiums, streets to recreational areas. The city of Shenzhen on China's southeastern coast is representative. The once sleepy fishing village of a million people was designated a "Special Economic Zone" by Chinese leader Deng Xiaoping in 1979. This meant the city could indulge in free-market activity with the rest of the world, welcoming foreign investment and joint partnerships.[8] It

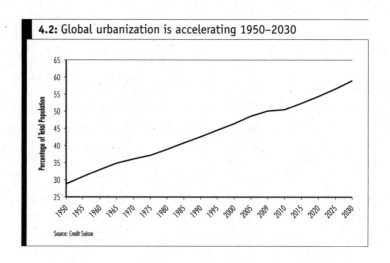

4.2: Global urbanization is accelerating 1950–2030

Source: Credit Suisse

didn't take long for the bulldozers and land scrapers to carve out a city that today boasts a population of about 10 million people who are engaged in Shenzhen's primary occupation of manufacturing. In addition to the many businesses in the city, Shenzhen has a stock exchange, an international trade centre and many colleges, universities and tourist sites.[9]

In 2008, Shenzhen's per capita income stood at US$13,153. That may be a tad high, or even a tad low but even if it's off by $1,000 either way it still makes it one of China's richest cities. More symbolically, it puts Shenzhen and its citizens in the "high income" category according to the World Bank, which benchmarks the group at US$12,196 or more.[10] Higher standards of living

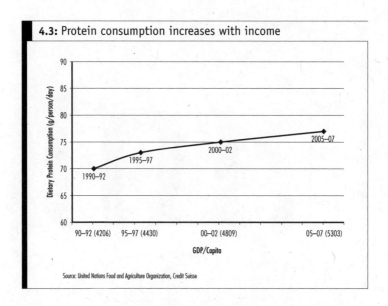

4.3: Protein consumption increases with income

Source: United Nations Food and Agriculture Organization, Credit Suisse

invariably lead to better, higher-protein diets. When people begin to earn more money, as many now do in Shenzhen and hundreds of other cities in developing countries, it becomes a personal priority to diversify away from starchy staples such as wheat and start consuming beef, chicken and pork. In other words, rice and beans don't cut it anymore. What was once considered too expensive is now becoming a mainstay among growing numbers of middle-class people thanks to incomes that have substantially risen since they left the farm to work in factories in China, the service sector in India and the oil wells of Russia.

Pork is the preferred, cultural choice in China, poultry in Russia, beef and veal in Brazil. In India the mainstay

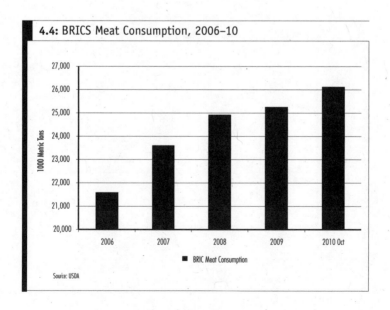

4.4: BRICS Meat Consumption, 2006–10

Source: USDA

is still vegetarian, which reflects both tradition and the
lowest per capita income of the BRICs.[11]

In China, pork production grew from 9 million tons
in 1978—the year economic reforms were announced—
to 46 million tons in 2003. China now accounts for half
of the world's total consumption of pork.[12] In Russia, 2%
of the world's population consumes 18% of the world's
chicken, and Brazil's 180 million people ate slightly less
than China's 1.4 billion.[13] And it takes an incredible
amount of grain to grow and feed livestock. A steer in
a feedlot requires about 7 kilograms of grain for each
kilogram of weight gain. For pork, each kilogram of

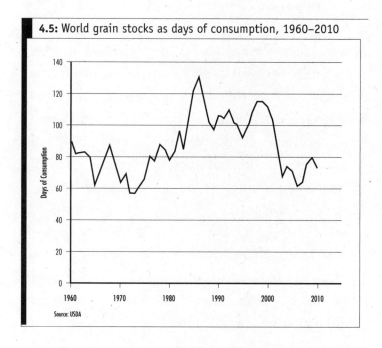

4.5: World grain stocks as days of consumption, 1960–2010

Source: USDA

additional live weight requires about 3.5 kilograms, and for poultry it's just over 2 kilograms.[14] This means the world's huge grain harvest is increasingly consumed as feed. Over 260 million acres of U.S. forest have been cleared in recent years for cropland to meet the world's increasingly meat-centred diet.

World grain stocks, or the amount of grain available as inventory for human consumption, peaked in the late 1980s at around 130 days. That's the number of days the world had as a cushion against poor harvests and to meet growing human and livestock demand. Today, the number of days has dropped below 80 days, a figure that leaves us one bad year away from trouble.

Another factor contributing to the loss of arable land stems from desertification. Rising numbers of grazing livestock destroy grasslands, leaving topsoil with nothing to anchor it against wind. In China, hundreds of thousands of hectares of potentially arable land have fallen victim to advancing deserts. In the country's Xinjiang autonomous region, the huge Taklamakan and the smaller Kumtag deserts are expanding and threaten to become one.[15] The same situation is unfolding on the southwestern edge of Inner Mongolia. In the U.S., 85% of topsoil loss is the result of livestock raising. In the Midwest, farmers are cultivating crops in only a few inches of topsoil.

Hand in hand with topsoil loss and advancing deserts is the concern about the availability of water to irrigate the world's crops. In 2003, the United Nations set the minimum water requirement per person at 50 litres per day: five for drinking, 20 for sanitation, 15 for bathing and 10 for food preparation. In comparison, it takes 2,000 litres of water—40 times as much—to produce the food we eat each day, with 70% of that directed toward irrigation and the remainder for livestock.[16] Historically, farmers were able to redirect river water to meet their needs. But demands have required the world to access water tables and aquifers. These are shrinking or, in the case of some aquifers, not being given enough time to replenish themselves. From India to China and the U.S., water tables and aquifers are being pumped dry. And although most people recognize the growing water shortfall, few make the leap to consider its impact on food production.

Of the world's three leading grains—rice, wheat and corn—which together account for 90% of the grain harvest, rice and wheat are grown almost entirely as food crop, with only one-sixth of the wheat harvest used to feed animals or make biofuel.[17] In contrast, the world's corn harvest is increasingly consumed by cars as biofuel, which has been mandated by the U.S. to stretch oil use for transportation. The 107 million tons of grain that went to U.S. ethanol distilleries in 2009 was enough to feed 330 million people for one year at average world consumption levels. More than 25% of the total U.S. grain crop was turned into ethanol to gas up cars last year. With 200 ethanol distilleries in the country set up to transform food into fuel, the amount of corn processed has tripled since 2004.[18] Increased demand for food to fuel Americans' commute to work and back puts additional pressures on world food supplies.

In addition to eating better, rising incomes spur car ownership. The previous chapter documented the rising number of cars sold in China. For every million cars, an estimated 20,000 hectares of land must be paved. In the U.S., where 0.07 hectares of paved land are paved for each car, every five cars requires the paving of an area the size of a football field. Thus the 2 million cars China added between 2005 and 2008 means the asphalting of an area equal to nearly 400,000 football fields.[19]

The competition between cars and crops for arable land may be the issue of the day, but looking farther out, rising populations are the greatest long-term concern. In 1950, there were 2.5 billion people in the world. In 2000, there were 6 billion. By 2050, global population is expected to rise to about 9 billion. With more than 70 million more people coming to the dinner table each year, it's getting harder and harder for the world's farmers to feed them.[20] Most of the growth is coming from developing countries as opposed to developed. In fact, the U.K., Japan and Germany are projected to have smaller populations by 2050, while countries such as India, China, Brazil, Mexico, Indonesia, Vietnam and Egypt are expecting big increases. The reason is simple. In pre-industrialized countries, births and deaths are both high

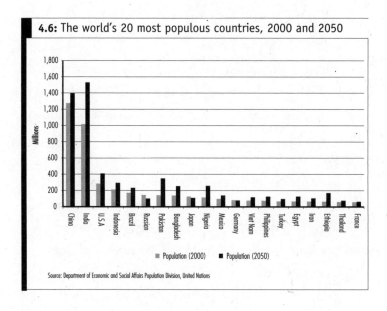

4.6: The world's 20 most populous countries, 2000 and 2050

■ Population (2000)   ■ Population (2050)

Source: Department of Economic and Social Affairs Population Division, United Nations

and relatively in balance. As countries grow economically, living standards and diets improve, as does health care. With birth rates remaining high and mortality rates dropping, populations begin to grow. This trend reverses itself over time as working adults have fewer children, women become more educated and productivity per person rises. The birth rate slows, eventually stabilizing with death rates. This cycle has been completed in most of the developed world. But it is just getting started in the developing world.[21]

Clearly, food supplies are going to come under intense pressure in the years to come due to fast-growing populations, city expansion and higher protein diets. But with fewer and fewer acres of arable land to farm, what's the answer? And how does the intersection of these trends impact the TSX? To answer the first question, we'll have to go back 150 years to find out about something called the Law of the Minimum, and then we'll fast-forward to the present to look at the impact on Canada's benchmark stock index.

Although the Romans knew enough about farming to recognize the importance of crop rotation, manure spreading and the liming of acidic soils, very little progress had been made over the years to fully understand the use of plant nutrients to aid plant growth. That changed in the mid-1800s when a chemist by the name of Justus Von Liebig got bored with organic chemistry and turned his attention to plant chemistry.[22] The body of work that preceded Liebig was modest at best.

A variety of scientists—German, English and French—had over the previous 300 years come to various conclusions regarding the importance of water and soil for plant growth. In one notable 17th-century experiment, a five-pound willow tree was planted in 200 pounds of soil. Five years later, the tree had grown to 169 pounds but the soil had lost but two ounces in weight. The water, it was concluded, was the only nutrient utilized by the tree for growth. In 1699, an Englishman by the name of John Woodward grew plants in four different containers. One held rain water, the other, water from the River Thames, the third was filled with Hyde Park effluent and the fourth, effluent mixed with garden mould. The plants that grew best were the ones with higher amounts of sediment in the water. Woodward, in this case, concluded that soil was the key.[23]

Liebig thought bigger. In 1840 he drew wide attention to agricultural fertility by suggesting chemical elements in the soil are the key to making things grow. Liebig's Law, or the Law of the Minimum, states that plant growth is controlled not by the total resources available in the soil but by the scarcest resource. In other words, if you increase all nutrients available to the plant, it does not increase growth. But if you increase the amount of the scarcest or limiting nutrient, then plant growth improves. To illustrate his point, Liebig used a wooden barrel two-thirds full with water. He then shortened one barrel stave and added more water. The shorter stave allowed the water to escape, highlighting the fact that total barrel capacity is limited to the length of the shortest stave. Plants, Liebig said, were similarly limited in their growth capacity by the nutrient in shortest supply in the soil.[24]

From that day forward, agricultural fertility took off due to its ability to improve crop yields and soil quality. The rule of thumb when it comes to the return on investment in crop nutrients is three to one. So for every dollar spent enriching crop fields farmers can expect a $3 return.[25] As a result, fertilizer is one of the most productive near-term solutions to ensure greater food security yet many regions around the world remain unfertilized.

There are 16 chemical elements that are essential for plant growth. Three of them—carbon, hydrogen and oxygen—are in the air while the rest—nitrogen, phosphorous, potassium and calcium, to name a few—are in soil.[26] Liebig, I must admit, is someone I'd never heard of until I met Darrin Maupin. Maupin had graduated near the top of his class at Boston College in 1998. I was still working hard to fill gaps in the Team Canada roster when I looked at his resume. I was impressed and gave him a call.

Maupin said he had accepted a job at Goldman Sachs and it was too late to consider a role on Team Canada. I persisted and asked him to lunch at Maison Robert in downtown Boston to talk things over. We ate outside as it was spring and the weather was spectacular. Over lunch, I explained to Maupin what I was doing with Team Canada and the opportunity that awaited him. After two hours, he said the job sounded perfect. He was convinced. But he had, in fact, signed back the offer. I told him I was willing to call Goldman and ask them to tear up the contract if he would be willing to join Team Canada. He said yes. I called Goldman later that day and Maupin joined the team.

I was glad he did. I didn't see the agriculture story. He did. In 2005, he came into my office talking stock stories related to agriculture. He pushed a book across my desk, *Outgrowing the Earth.* I read it that night and although the tone is alarmist and shrill, the book presents interesting thoughts on global food security and touches on many of the themes I articulated earlier in this chapter. I ordered copies of the book for the rest of the team and my long-term views of agriculture and its investment potential were set as the notion of raising crop productivity ranked as one of humankind's most important priorities.

That wasn't the case in Liebig's age. There was plenty of arable land available and no real need to boost productivity. This changed dramatically after the Second World War when a wide range of countries started industrializing and millions of people started migrating from farms to cities. The fertilizer industry, which Liebig unknowingly started, underwent terrific growth from 1950 to 1989 with fertilizer use climbing from 14 million to 146 million tons.[27]

Fertilizer use dipped in the 1990s as the Soviet Union and its satellite countries fell. They had enjoyed government subsidies to buy fertilizer and when market prices came into effect, few farmers could afford it. After these countries' economies stabilized, fertilizer sales grew again and have since taken off led by the buying giants of China, India and Brazil. Fertilizer consumption measured by kilograms per hectare of arable land has shown marked increases over the past four decades. In China, 458 kilograms per hectare were used in 1971 compared to 3,311 in 2007. In India the numbers have moved from 166 kilograms to 1,422 over the same period. And Brazil consumed 303 kilograms in 1971 versus 1,901 in 2007.[28] The reason fertilizer use has risen and will continue

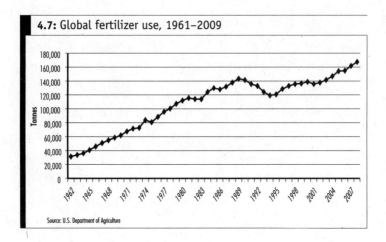

4.7: Global fertilizer use, 1961–2009

Source: U.S. Department of Agriculture

to rise is its impact on yields. Earlier we discussed the importance of grains—wheat, rice, corn and soybeans—in the global food supply chain for feeding people, livestock and now cars. Largely as a result of fertilizer, yields of all grains have jumped markedly over the past 40 years.

One of the key elements in fertilizer that makes grains grow best—or the one nutrient lacking as Liebig would say—is potassium. The grain family of crops is the heaviest user of potassium and potassium is the chemical element found in potash. And Canada has the largest, most accessible potash deposits in the world, which brings us to the investment potential in agriculture and its leading role in the boom.

Potash is a general term covering several types of potassium salts of which the most important is potassium chloride. Roughly 95% of world potash production goes into fertilizer with the other 5% directed to commercial

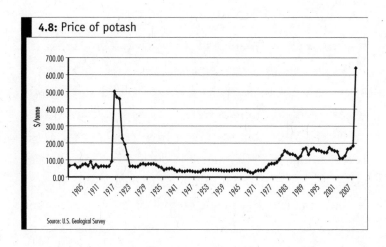

4.8: Price of potash

Source: U.S. Geological Survey

and industrial applications. The province of Saskatchewan is rich with potash deposits, which are mined at depths of about 3,000 feet below ground in the southern end of the province. Conservatively, Saskatchewan could supply world demand at current levels for several hundred years.[29]

The province's competitive advantage in potash production is the extent and quality of its reserves. They lie in flat beds allowing for easy mining, which translates into some of the lowest production costs in the world. Only 5% of the total Canadian potash mined is used in the country with the remainder consumed by the U.S., China, Brazil and the Pacific Rim countries of Japan, Korea and Indonesia.[30] In total, over 150 countries use potash for crops but it is produced in only about a dozen of them. In other words, it's scarce. World production totalled 36 million metric tons in 2008, with Canada the leading producer.

As potash consumption rose through the 2000s, prices soared. At their peak in 2008, potash was selling for nearly US$1,000 a tonne. That figure fell to US$350 by the end of the year as the financial crisis took hold and farmers, uncertain of the impact from the crisis, restrained their purchases. Withholding potash from cropland for a year is something most farmers can do without jeopardizing yield, but after that, croplands start losing efficiency, so it's only a matter of time before potash purchases resume. That's what happened in 2010 as prices began to reverse course with the signing of new sales contracts. Canpotex, a Saskatchewan-based potash co-op that establishes prices, has posted on its website a price of US$413 a tonne for granular grade as of March 2010. Potash Corp., based in Saskatchewan, controls the largest reserve and was the company that formed Canpotex. It's like the OPEC of potash. They take control of the global marketing and negotiating of potash prices and try to stabilize them by managing supply.

Potash Corp. is an incredibly well-run company and will be a major powerhouse as time unfolds. It's a big weight on the Toronto Stock Exchange and its growth in share price over the past 10 years is impressive.

Other important fertilizers are nitrogen and phosphate. The latter is in extremely short supply. The total amount of extractable phosphate is expected to peak around 2030, at which time demand will overtake supply. Over time, phosphate depletion has averaged 2% a year, but in 2008 it jumped by a record 7%—driven mainly by China.[31] This has led to a spike in phosphate prices with it commanding a price significantly higher in 2008 than it did in 2007. The one company in Canada that does have exposure to a wider variety of fertilizers—including phosphate—is Agrium. It too is a big weight on the index and that weight will be felt in the coming years as the boom gains momentum.

Recognizing the growing importance of fertilizer to meet rising food demands and the high returns on equity have led to a large number of takeovers and mergers in the agricultural sector. The summer of 2010 saw Australia's BHP Billiton Ltd. launch an unsolicited takeover bid for Potash Corp. to the tune of US$38.56 billion. Potash called the unsolicited offer "grossly inadequate" and triggered a poison pill defence to ward off the Melbourne-based company. Billiton and Vale SA, the world's two biggest mining companies, have already spent a combined US$4.9 billion in 2010 on fertilizer acquisitions to get a slice of the huge profits from potash. Melbourne-based Billiton bought Canada's Athabasca Potash Inc., while Vale scooped up a 16% stake in a Brazilian fertilizer business. Billiton has also earmarked US$10 billion to develop the Jansen potash project in Saskatchewan, while a total of 28 other projects—some early, some mid-stage—are underway in the province. Agrium, meanwhile, has been in a tussle with three other firms bidding on the assets of fertilizer-maker Terra

Industries. I think you're going to see more mergers and acquisitions activity as the boom unfolds and the resulting exuberance will be the last tailwind behind the boom.

In addition to the investment potential in fertilizer companies, a large number of other subsidiary and ancillary businesses are poised to benefit, such as livestock processors, agriculture equipment makers and grain transporters. Canadian Pacific, for instance, is a big transporter of grain and fertilizer, while you have other companies that store agricultural products and others that trade them and these are all public, so there's a big associative effect in the sector.

Other more subtle opportunities lie in farmland in Saskatchewan. There really aren't any places in the world that are as agriculturally blessed. There's unlimited water, plenty of land and world-class infrastructure already in place for shipping, storing and other services. There are very few places in the developed world that enjoy such a combination—one that could grow more attractive as productive farmland comes under pressure from a variety of sources. In the U.S. heartland where farming is king, there is concern over water and its long-term availability. Heartland water comes from a large aquifer that has been pumped hard for 70 years, whereas Canada has an abundance of water. The investment story on ag in Canada is not just the fertilizers, but also the transporters, equipment makers and the knock-on effect for farmers and local economies. That knock-on effect in itself is part of the boom. Boom creates boom.

And we're starting to see that in Saskatchewan land prices. Investors from around the world—Australia, the U.S. and the U.K.—are starting to buy huge chunks. A 324 hectare farm selling for $2 million, for example. A couple of years ago, the price would've been $600,000 according to historical comparisons.[32] Aside from the boom potential, the other driver behind soaring farm prices was a change in ownership rules by the Saskatchewan government. Until recently, only provincial residents were permitted to buy farmland—an attempt to preserve the family farm. The law kept prices artificially low, so now you're seeing them come up to real market value. I actually tried to buy some Saskatchewan farmland and a friend of mine did buy a 2,000 acre farm. He plans to rent the property and sell it down the road. A long-term investment in agriculture is how he sees it.

Whether it's Saskatchewan land, fertilizer companies, transporters or equipment makers, the investment opportunity in agriculture is broad, but it all narrows when you look at the Toronto Stock Exchange. And I'm not really sure Canadians can see how blessed they are to be at the centre of the universe in terms of ag, particularly fertilizer. The country and its companies are going to play a huge role in meeting the food challenge that comes from industrialization, population growth and the desire for better diets in developing countries.

With a better understanding of the boom potential behind agriculture, gold and oil, it's time to move on to the financial crisis of 2008. It proved to be an important stress test for my boom theory. And every indicator suggests the crisis was but an interruption in the long-term secular boom for our three leading players.

CHAPTER FIVE

Boom interrupted

And Then There Were None
Agatha Christie, 1939

I ronically, the biggest financial story of the decade didn't even make the front pages of the world's business press on the morning of Monday, September 15, 2008. Lehman Brothers filed for bankruptcy protection at 1:45 a.m. and Merrill Lynch, perhaps the best-known brand on Wall Street, had also sold itself to Bank of America in the early morning hours. But due to the timing of the bankruptcy and sale, the day's papers had long been printed and were being dropped on doorsteps, newsstands and offices as events were still unfolding.

The Lehman bankruptcy—the largest in U.S. history—spelled the end for the firm after it had toughed it out since 1850: through the crash of 1929, two world wars and countless recessions. Merrill, no flyweight by any measure, and its "thundering herd" of 17,000 brokers had been sold for about US$50 billion—about half of what it was worth 12 months earlier.[1] The weekend news printed that Monday morning was but the latest failure or rescue of an ever-growing number of big financial firms. Back in June 2007, two Bear Stearns hedge funds got the ball rolling when they ran out of cash and collapsed due to their exposure to the subprime market, or rotten mortgages. By March 2008, Bear itself had to stave off bankruptcy with help from the Fed, which came to the rescue assuming the company's bad debts but made the firm sell itself to JP Morgan Chase for US$2 a share, down from highs of about US$170.[2] One week before the Lehman announcement, the U.S. Treasury Department took over Fannie Mae and Freddie Mac—two government-sponsored enterprises that own or back US$5.3 trillion in mortgages—for US$100 billion each.[3]

As unrattling as the Lehman and Merrill news was for the markets, there was a looming sense that more shoes were about to drop. Insurance giant American International Group (AIG) had already asked the Fed for US$40 billion to get through the week.[4] Washington Mutual, the country's largest savings and loan company, was teetering and there were rumours that Wachovia, Citigroup and Morgan Stanley would be next. When the bell rang every Friday at market close, you wondered what new obituary was going to be written.

It was like Russian roulette every weekend for the first three quarters of 2008. The chamber was turning and you didn't know if there was going to be a bullet for another financial services company. It was, in effect, just like the great bank runs of the 1930s. We weren't seeing lines in front of banks like we saw in pictures from the '30s, but trust me, from an institutional perspective, it was a bank run. Big institutions were going online instead of getting in line to take their money out of these investment banks, brokers and insurers that had lost the trust of their lenders and top clients. Hedge fund clients were dropping investment banks from their approved lists. It was the silent, 21st-century equivalent of the 1930s bank runs in a computerized world.

If the way it quietly transpired made it eerie, what made it frightening was that we thought that years of regulation, socialization, and safety nets had made bank runs a thing of the past. But the human condition hadn't changed. We had just found another more up-to-date version. It was an e-bank run that took the form of people refusing to trade with Lehman and demanding their money back—no different than the unwinding we had seen in the 1930s. It was motivated by the same giant fear of not getting your money back. And when you demand cash back from these levered institutions, you only hope you're the first one asking, because you know there isn't enough in the till to pay everyone out. Remember the scene from Frank Capra's iconic film *It's a Wonderful Life*? It was like that, but instead of scared people demanding their money from a teller at the Bailey Building and Loan as they did in the movie, it was being played out with the silent whisper of computers. That's what I teach the kids in my Fed class at Tufts. The 2008 financial crisis got a lot of funky names and whatnot, but it was just a plain old bank run. People and institutions saying, "I want my money, and I want to get it before you get it, because if I don't get it soon, there won't be enough left," just as they had said in bank runs past.

The Lehman bankruptcy was pivotal in the crisis because it marked the first time bond investors were wiped out. To put that into context, if you're an equity guy like me, you don't want to be wiped out, but you will over the course of a career be down 20%, sometimes 40%. It happens. A wipeout shouldn't happen but it does. Now, let's move up the balance sheet a bit. Let's say you're a junk bond or subordinated debt investor. You've lost 10%, maybe you've lost some more, but like an equity guy, you're used to the volatility. You're playing in this arena.

Let's move up one more rung on the balance sheet. You're a bond investor, an investment-grade bond investor. You think you're first in line to be paid. You think. You're investing in things that the ratings agencies have told you are investment grade and the chance of default minuscule. Unlike the equity guys, you're used to losing, at the max, 2% to 3% of an investment. Maybe you blew your interest rate prediction and you lost a little. But default? Never. If you do, you really screwed up. I mean, *really* screwed up because you don't have defaults in this area.

Ratchet it up again: you're a money market investor who is lending money for a week. If you're really out there, you're lending money for three weeks, and you're lending this money to triple-A companies. So you say, "I'm lending you, General Electric, money for two weeks. I'm going to do a huge analysis. Okay, good! I did it! You've been around for 150 years. Two weeks, you've got billions on the balance sheet. Okay. I'll lend you the money." And then in 2008, even lending to these triple-A companies, you get no return. Imagine you're the money market guy and you walk in Monday morning and hear Lehman is gone, so you don't get anything back.

Money market guys never lose—it's just a question of how little they get in return. But this time around, they got zero. They lost everything. These are people that have never contemplated these levels of risk. The reason the system ground to a halt was that the money market guys barred the doors to their house, went into the basement and said, "I'm only lending to the government, Exxon or five other companies on the planet that I deem safe, and only for a week. And you know what? I won't lend to you, Goldman Sachs, or you, Morgan Stanley, because I just lost 100 cents on the dollar to Lehman. I'm taking my money and I'm putting it under the mattress. I'm putting it in treasury bills." It's insane, but it's the mass psychology of people running around with their heads cut off, and it wasn't just the money market guys that were losing their cool. I can tell you that their bosses came to the money market guys' offices and said, "If you lose me any amount of money, you're fired the next second. Are we clear?" So they stopped lending. They took the money they would usually roll over every 20 or 30 days and they were told, "Shrink it down to a week or less, and upgrade your portfolio to the government or Exxon, or maybe the Royal Bank." Only the most creditworthy customers in the world.

Put yourself in their shoes. Would you bet your career on anyone short of the most creditworthy in the world? So that was it, our modern-day system broken. It turned into a run on the bank. One of the big market rumours was that General Electric was a week away from failing because they didn't make the lists of the money market guys. Big companies like GE that have finance arms have to roll over debt every week, and it's huge amounts. Usually it would have been nothing for GE to get these vast sums, you wouldn't have thought twice about it. Another two weeks for GE? Sure, why not? But when the system broke, GE tried holding their regular auction and no one showed up. And that's why Lehman was pivotal leading us into the spiral. People realized things can blow up and go to zero.

That's when it hit people like a two-by-four coming down between their eyes and their response was, "I cannot lend to you, you or you." That's how dire the situation had become and every weekend it got worse. It was building and building with failures and bailouts. Bear Stearns wasn't actually that bad when you look back because none of the bondholders lost anything. Bear Stearns was one of those good bailouts, in a sense. The equity holders lost almost everything, but the bondholders still got 100 cents on the dollar. It wasn't until Lehman and then savings and loan giant Washington Mutual (WaMu) that the Federal Deposit Insurance Corporation (FDIC) let bondholders go.

They lost it. I don't think they let super senior money markets go, but the subordinated bondholders got nothing. So people who were used to getting back, worst case, 95 cents on the dollar, got zero, but it wasn't until Lehman that the guys who always got 100 cents back on the dollar got zero that was everyone got whacked. And a money market mutual fund broke the buck because of its Lehman paper. The Fed in Boston sensed a major run on money market funds as a result. So it wasn't like Lehman was done and you could say, "Ah, thank goodness. At least it's over." When Lehman went, Merrill was suspected to be next. The same was true for AIG. No one knew exactly how bad it was for those two, but everyone knew they were right in the middle of this thing and there were plenty of European banks to focus on, too, that were very much in doubt.

If the Fed, the Treasury and all those other guys hadn't taken extraordinary measures, you would have seen a repeat of the 1930s. If you were living in the States, your local bank at the corner would have been fine because you've got FDIC and your deposits up to US$100,000 are insured, but it would have been these behemoth financials like Goldman, it would have been Merrill, and it would have been AIG that got vapourized. It might have taken Citigroup at some point.

And it wasn't until we got to that point that U.S. Federal Reserve Chairman Ben Bernanke saw the analogy between the bank runs of today and those of yesterday. By the end of September—after WaMu had officially cratered and people were actually lining up at the doors to take their money—Bernanke was in front of the big thinkers of Congress trying to convince them of the wisdom behind the US$700 billion bailout proposal.

"I spent my career as an academic studying great depressions," the former Princeton professor stated calmly. "I can tell you from history that if we don't act in a big way, you can expect another great depression, and this time it is going to be far, far worse."[5]

Words which turned into deeds as we shall see.

I couldn't help thinking the bond guys were right. It was spring 2008 and I was meeting with two members of the asset allocation committee in my office. As CIO, I was the head of the committee whose main responsibility was assessing and changing "allocations" or amounts of stocks, bonds and cash across the Fidelity balanced funds product lineup, which includes the flagship $10-billion Fidelity Canadian Asset Allocation Fund.

Balanced funds get their name from the balance of three assets the fund can invest in: stocks, bonds and cash. If, for instance, we believe there is a good chance that stocks will do well over a coming period of time, we could adjust the "balance" of the fund and buy more stocks and sell bonds. Alternatively, if we believe bonds have a better chance of performing well, we could decrease our exposure to stocks and buy more bonds. Cash, the third component, could similarly rise and fall depending on our view.

Fidelity Canadian Asset Allocation Fund is the country's largest, and the committee would meet regularly to review its allocations. But in light of the rumblings coming from the market and the Bear Stearns hedge fund blow-up, we found ourselves meeting more often. Particularly troubling were the messages being sent by a chart I regularly monitor. The chart shows the spread between corporate and government bonds and it was widening like I'd never seen. The "spread" or difference between the rates of interest paid on bonds issued by companies and those issued by the government can telegraph important signals as to the nature of risk in the marketplace. With the spread rising higher to never before seen lengths, investors were basically saying they wanted higher premiums if they were going to lend companies money. There were also rising numbers of credit default swaps (CDS)—a form of credit protection for the buyer in exchange for a guarantee of creditworthiness by the seller—was also rising.

Having managed balanced fund and asset allocation products since 1986, I knew exactly the moves to take: sell stocks in favour of bonds and reduce riskier assets.

We would rotate out of certain sectors and move into others while building our bond component. I remember thinking I might be off by a quarter, but that didn't bother me. I wanted to get ahead of it. We also started to reduce commodity exposure. Not only was the market telling us to do it, but commodities tend to trade off in the summer, so that was further motivation. We were below in the spring and we were saying we were going to keep reducing or hold off because the time to re-buy commodities is the fall. So we were not only acting on the crisis as it unfolded, but we were also unwinding because commodities had peaked in July 2007 at about the same time as the Dow. We were coming off and not expecting to get back into commodities in a big way until after the subsequent summer, so the fall of '08, and then things started to come undone and we kept going down below market weight.

The move to a more conservative asset allocation seemed prescient in light of the dominoes that had fallen throughout the year. And it looked smarter as the days went by. By November, the Dow had fallen to its lowest point in a decade, wiping out trillions of dollars of wealth. By making that early move, our asset allocation products performed better relative to our peers. But lost money is lost money.

By the spring 2009, the markets in Canada and the United States had fallen to such a degree that a generational buying opportunity was in the offing. The

TSX was 30% to 40% oversold, the Dow somewhat less so, but still, oversold is oversold. The moment was screaming for us to zig because the rest of the world was zagging. Buy weakness, sell strength, as the old saying goes. To me the opportunity couldn't be more obvious. But business and mainstream media couldn't resist the headlines and the overarching message was to sell everything and move to cash.

Over the past 100 years, we had been under the trendline by 30% only once or twice. I asked myself if there was anything else I needed to know. Short of Canada becoming a communist country or some

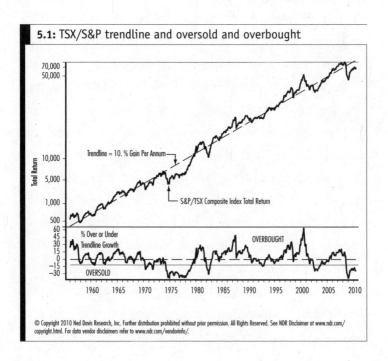

5.1: TSX/S&P trendline and oversold and overbought

dramatic change in the human condition, you have to assume things will revert back to normal.

That was the message I was delivering in February and March 2009 to anyone who was listening. At presentations to advisors, I would throw the trendline chart up on the screen highlighting the variance of return since 1972 and how far below it we currently stood. I said we were at a generational buy for Canadian equities and asked the audience to name reasons why we wouldn't return to normalcy, why things would be different this time. Assuming everyone is still out there working hard, being creative and making things, the answer should be, "It won't be different this time." By the first-quarter 2009, the indicators were screaming "buy."

In addition to the extraordinary moment the markets had given us for a buying opportunity, I also knew the boom had simply been interrupted. It was alive and well and the proof lay in the answers to two questions. The first was whether we had created enough supply to meet demand in the areas of gold, oil and agriculture, because all booms end with supply being created. Since the boom started in 2000, gold had cracked the US$1,000 an ounce, oil had climbed to above US$140 a barrel and fertilizer—notably potash—was selling for more about US$1,000 a tonne, which was a record. Everything had moved up and in the world of commodities, rising prices attracts capital, which spurs exploration, development and extraction to take advantage of the favourable pricing environment.

We saw this unfolding in each sector—gold, oil and agriculture—through the 2000s but no new supplies had come on stream and that, to me, was the big tipoff. Take the U.S. housing market as the most recent example of a boom ending due to a huge influx of supply. We had years of outsize housing growth. That was a boom alright, but the reason it came to an end lay in the fact that we had builders constructing record numbers of homes and condos.

This is what happened to gold and oil in 1980 and 1981. That was the end of the "things-that-go-bump-in-the-night" boom. Prices for gold and oil went up like crazy but supply came on to meet demand. We found a lot of oil and we found a lot of gold. That's an important part of the continuing gold and oil booms because we didn't find any of this stuff over the course of the 2000s. When oil hit US$140, you didn't find a lot of oil. You didn't add a lot of supply. It was there for a very brief time. It's harder and harder to find this stuff. You didn't find any gold either. The gold supply has actually fallen.

With no change in the supply side of the equation, the next question to ask is whether the demand dynamic had changed. Within six months of the U.S. unveiling its US$700-billion Troubled Asset Relief Program, or TARP, to save its financial and banking systems, the BRICs and a wide range of developing countries had gotten up off the canvas and were on solid footing, which further confirmed my boom thesis. According to the IMF and as at July 2010, China's real GDP growth is expected to end the year at 10.5%; for India it's 9.4% and for Brazil, 7.1%. Russia is the forecast laggard coming in at 4.3%. In comparison, the U.S. is estimated to finish the year at 3.3%, while Germany and France will reach 1.4% and the U.K. 1.2%. Canada, interestingly, is anticipated to outpace its G7 peers, notching real GDP of 3.6% for 2010.[6]

Looking ahead, the IMF sees developing countries growing anywhere from three to four times faster than the G7 economies in 2011 with China predicted to hit 9.6% and India 8.4%.[7] Overall, the path of industrialization through regulatory reform, economic restructuring and

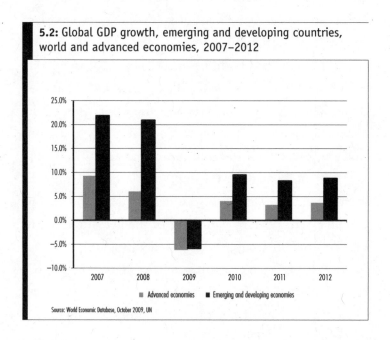

5.2: Global GDP growth, emerging and developing countries, world and advanced economies, 2007–2012

Source: World Economic Database, October 2009, UN

institutional change had left the developing world in a healthier position than the developed countries to weather the financial crisis.

The quick resurgence in growth among the BRICs tells me they are "decoupling" from economic dependence on the rich countries of the world. In particular, they were decoupling from the United States. Cycles of output, consumption and investment generally become more closely correlated between countries over time.[8] That has happened among the developing and BRIC economies as evidenced by China and India. But when you look at the cycles between the Western economies and the BRICs, they're diverging.

The reasons vary as to why. The most important is that most developing countries and their banking systems had very little exposure to the toxic assets that ate up Wall Street in the first place, so there was less trouble for them to get into—not unlike Canada. Size is another important component. When credit markets seized and consumers stopped buying in industrialized countries, the Chinese and Indian giants could turn inwards, relying on domestic consumers to absorb manufacturing output. State banks, which in India's case hold 70% of all bank assets, had plenty of money in the till to loan.[9] This negated any need to tap foreign banks or the stock market. These are alternatives that Western economies have always relied on but were unavailable to them this time around.

Due to the BRICs' and other developing markets' stronger growth paths, they will increasingly land on the radars of global investors who, looking to make a buck, will have to choose between a the much slower growth of the U.S. or Europe—traditional fishing holes—or faster growth in India, China and on down the line to Vietnam, Thailand and Indonesia. This choice underscores developing countries' value potential. It's both a nod to longer-term robustness in the developing world and a confirmation that the old countries may be showing their age.

So for reasons unique to the BRICs, they were in a much better position to resume their upward, pre-financial crisis trajectory, which brings us back to my two questions. Did we create enough new supply? Or has demand been curtailed to such a degree that it requires less supply? Based on what I've seen across the globe, the answer to both questions is "No," which means the boom has only been interrupted. I'll take that thought another step and say the boom has been fortified by the actions taken by central bankers across the globe to staunch the credit crisis. What they did, in fact, was pour gasoline into the mix—gasoline in the form of zero or near-zero interest rates in every developed country but Australia, budget deficits as far as the eye can see and stimulus packages from Washington to Beijing. And the gasoline is slowly moving toward the burning truck just like you see in the movies.

And the gasoline is going to keep flowing for some time. Whether by good luck or divine intervention, you've got Ben Bernanke, one of the two most-renowned Depression scholars of all time, running the Fed. And interestingly, up until the Lehman bankruptcy and liquidation, he exuded the same hesitancy as the Fed at the start of the Great Depression to kick his action plan into high gear. It was the same type of delay as during the Depression when the guys on the Board of Governors started lowering interest rates. People always think, "Well, Hoover just went on vacation," and whatnot. But the Board of Governors was lowering rates at a fast pace. In hindsight, they just weren't watching the indicators they should have. They were too focused on simply lowering rates. Moreover, they had come through a serious recession in 1920 by following similar steps.

"What do you want from me? I'm getting right down to 1%," was the refrain, "Rates have never been this low. Shouldn't that fix the problem?" And those who study the Depression say, "Well, okay, but you still totally messed it up. It wasn't about the rates; it was about having cash on hand in the banks." It was about the real rates. Real rates are measured as the difference between the observed rate and the inflation rate. Deflation was running at 10% (think of this as −10% inflation), so real rates were 11%. The Fed governors didn't look at those things at the time. They were also hamstrung by their official playbook: to adhere to the gold standard, they were occasionally forced to raise rates to keep gold in the country. But a guy who really knows what they did wrong happens to be in the Fed chair now. He came in and did 12 things never done before because they were just the opposite of the screwups of the 1930s.

But up until Lehman, the Fed was following the same script that played out in the Depression. They lowered rates incrementally; they were talking up a good game. Bernanke was on TV as late as the middle of 2007 saying, "Well, the housing thing's pretty much blown through. It's fine. We're expecting strong recovery next year so we've lowered rates by 25 basis points." If you go back and read the Fed minutes from 1930 or '31, it's the same kind of stuff: "Oh, look, we had an increase in February and rates are low, so we're expecting that to hold and we're going to be booming, and we ought to be worried about sticking to our low-rate policy."

So yes, we have exactly the right person at the Fed to avoid a repeat of the Depression, but everything has a cost and unforeseen consequences—that's just the nature of life. I believe the price we'll pay will be a Fed that stays too loose, too long because they're still fighting the battle of 1930–1940. Something very rarely taught about the Depression and that I teach in my class the 1937–38 recession, also known as the Roosevelt Recession. Unless you really get into the nuts and bolts, everyone says the Depression lasted from 1929 to the war, but actually it hit bottom in 1932. Roosevelt came in and enacted all this fiscal stimulus, not unlike Obama throwing money at everything, but back then it was new. Roosevelt targeted an unprecedented amount of federal deficit spending toward individuals, and the Fed had taken rates down to zero. Roosevelt also took us off the gold standard so we no longer had to worry about that thing, the dollar was devalued, which we've tried to do in recent times as best we can, and between 1932 and 1936, GDP grew at a compounded rate of roughly 12% a year. Unemployment went from 25% down to a better 12%. It still wasn't good, it was still the Depression, but the price of commodities started to increase in value over the next four years.

At that point, the Fed and Roosevelt thought, "Maybe we ought to worry a little bit about overheating." So late in '36, Roosevelt announced a series of presumably inconsequential tax increases—minor tax increases and mostly on the wealthy—because the government was running a big budget deficit that led people, primarily on the Republican side, to say that all this spending was irresponsible. At the same time, the Fed started to raise rates by increasing reserve requirements—their favoured tool at the time. There were a lot of free, unused reserves in the banking system, so the Fed increased reserve requirements just a little bit. They didn't actually take any money out of the system, they just decided to be a bit cautious by saying that these weren't free reserves anymore, they were a reserve requirement. It was a bookkeeping change.

Within six months, the U.S. economy went into a severe recession, the third or fourth worst recession in the history of the country, from 1937 to '39. Unemployment went back from 12% to 20% and GDP fell another 15% pretty quickly. And the U.S. stock market went down dramatically from that point as well.

What's the take-away from this story?

Bernanke knows this stuff a lot better than I do and I believe he's worried about re-enacting the Roosevelt Recession. So he's going to pay a lot of lip service to raising rates and talking tough—"Oh, I'm a hawk. Look at the shiny discount rate I raised over here"—but in his heart of hearts I think he's going to wait longer than is prudent to raise rates and stop printing money because he's got that recession of '37 imprinted on him. It's imprinted on the Obama Administration as well, because Christina Romer, the outgoing Chair of the Council of Economic Advisers and co-author of the 2008 economic recovery plan, has talked about the recession of '37 as a guidepost. If you didn't hear about it, that's because it didn't get any mainstream press coverage. This is one of those geeky things that are not today's excitement.

So part of my Boom Interrupted thesis is a government and Fed driving with their eyes on the rear-view mirror looking at 1937. Generals are always fighting the last war, and I think we have the most brilliant general in Bernanke, who knows everything about the last war. That's my point. Milton Friedman's dead, so you can't pick him, and your number two pick is Bernanke the Depression scholar, so he's going to fight that war. Just imagine a guy, an academic star from Princeton University, who studies one thing all his life and then he's put into a role where he can leverage that knowledge. Well, what's he going to do? He's got his papers, he's got his dissertations, he's got his econometric models. He built it all already, he's going to use it and he isn't going to mess it up. He'll mess up something else, but he's not going to mess up this.

And are there any politicians around who can't convince themselves overspending is the righteous thing to do? That's not a hard sell with any politician, left or right, especially if you're presented with a bunch of academic mumbo-jumbo that tells you, "Not only do you have to spend, but if you look at history, you have to spend beyond what seems at all prudent. That's the righteous thing to do."

It may be the right thing to do, but imagine if it isn't. What will the consequences be if they stay short at low rates too long? We're already running deficits like we've never seen before (other than in the middle of the Second World War), and they only promise to go up now that Obama got his Obamacare.

And it's not just the U.S. that's taking this approach to their economic maladies. Virtually all the developed world is charging down the same path blazed by John Maynard Keynes, the British star economist of the 1940s whose views on economic policy coming out of the Great

Depression gathered widespread attention. Keynes, unlike most of his ilk, argued for more government spending, accommodative rate policies and a willingness to take on debt and deficits to ensure full employment in good times and bad. Keynes may be long dead and buried, but his economic medicine is being doled out across the world in amounts he would've been happy to see. What if he and his disciples are wrong? Some cracks showed in the Keynesian model in the late 1960s and early 1970s when stagflation hit the scene. Stagflation was not thought possible under Keynes' approach, but it happened all the same. And now Japan: Japan has been trying to dig itself out of perpetual deflation and slow growth for the past 20 years, and they've been following a Keynesian script. Is it possible the U.S. and the U.K. will end up in the same quicksand?

I don't know, but at some point, you're going to get this combination of incredibly expansionary monetary and fiscal stimulus meeting the explosive demand from developing economies. This will overwhelm the loss of demand from the developed world and continue for many years to come. We don't know when we'll cross that line, but when we do, you'd better be invested, because the printing of money, the deficits and the stimulus packages—collectively called quantitative easing—all bode well for the boom in gold, oil and agriculture.

If—and it's a big if—the G20 countries embrace true fiscal austerity as they pledged in Toronto and if they are willing to expose themselves to the political fallout—riots in the streets, strikes and civil disruption—that still doesn't address the other side of the equation, which is monetary discipline. In fact, I think the European Central Bank (ECB) would rather buy EU country debt, monetize it and stay accommodative instead of inflicting pain across Europe.

After all, money printing is something the European Central Bank, the Bank of England and the U.S. had gotten very good at by the late 2000s. They're all printing it out of thin air to help jump-start their economies. Following the Second World War, the answer to Europe's debt problems lay in growth with inflation. That strategy is still page one in their playbook, as it is in the States. The challenge is growth. The U.S., the U.K. and others didn't just stumble down the recession hill, they fell, so they're going to continue to prime the pump. When central banks start printing money, it triggers the three-step process I mentioned in the gold chapter: the monetary base gets pumped up, the money supply increases lead to inflation and then inflation leads to higher gold prices. The financial crisis has unleashed trillions of dollars across the developed world—led by the U.S.—adding more fuel to the fire for higher gold prices for years to come because money supply is highly correlated with inflation, as illustrated earlier.

That's one of the key reasons why there will be a gold boom. It's not because people have a price in mind, it's because they see there's no discipline on the monetary or fiscal side. Money supply growth has always led to inflation, inflation has always led to gold, and this time around, the stakes are the biggest ever.

I don't want this to be a book on inflation, but it's almost inevitable that we'll see some inflation result from governments printing all this money. When that inflation will arrive is open to debate, but sometime around 2011 or 2012 we should see an uptick in the consumer price index (CPI). It's a key element of the Boom Interrupted story with regard to gold because monetary expansion has always led to inflation.

Finally, big government deficits in conjunction with large stimulus packages are generating new demand in a big way. This is really the icing on the cake. Governments everywhere—from the U.S. to Germany to China—are running deficits and offering cash for clunkers. That's stimulating demand everywhere but most notably in developing markets. We've probably semi-permanently lost some demand for stuff in the U.S. and Europe. We're not going back to the pre-crisis (2006) days of selling 17 million cars in the U.S. and building 1.5 million houses. That was credit-induced nonsense. We took out some demand for stuff when we did that, which we might stabilize with our largess, but a lot of that money that the world is printing is going to end up in India and China and Brazil and it's going to reinvigorate their demand. They've got two things going for them. They have GDP growth and they have per capita consumption growth added to what was already a strong surge.

That growth is the big reason behind the post-interruption rise in oil prices. They've already rebounded sharply from the lows they hit when the financial sector blew up. After a quick drop to US$34 a barrel at the close of 2008, oil jumped back to about US$70 a barrel in the summer of 2009. That's one big bounce. And prices have remained there right into 2010. What does that tell you? It should tell you that all those big factories in China that slowed production after the financial crisis are back running 24/7. The ports are busy, the cargo ships full. In 2009 and 2010, when oil demand in most of the world shrank, China was the only major economy to see strong growth with its oil consumption rising. Predictions for 2011 and beyond are well above that. India, Brazil and other developing countries are also returning to or surpassing previous oil consumption levels.

The bounce also tells you the price of oil is no longer correlated to the economies of the U.S., Germany and Japan. There was a time when oil prices would rise and fall on the backs of these countries' economic growth or lack of it. Strong growth for these three meant higher oil prices; lacklustre growth meant lower prices. If you use the 10-year bond rates in the U.S (3%), Germany (2%) and Japan (1%) as a gauge of current growth, however, you'd think the world had come to an end because they're so low. And yet oil remains about US$70 to $80 a barrel, which goes back to my introductory comments about the importance of looking at the world through a different lens. The U.S. is no longer the centre of the universe, nor is Japan, nor is Germany. If they were, the price of a barrel of oil would be closer to US$10 as opposed to US$80.

The demand side of the oil story is intact thanks to the developing world. And demand should get stronger as we enter the next phase of the up cycle. Cast your mind forward to the day when the battered and bruised economies of the United States and Europe start recovering by making up for bought petroleum. When that will happen I don't know, but it should give oil another kick as weak economies resume their plodding growth. Meantime, new oil reserves will still be far away, so current oil supplies will once again struggle to catch up to quickening demand.

Of the three leading industries in the boom, agriculture is the laggard coming off the 2008 bottom. The one exception in ag is wheat, which has made a stunning upward move during the summer of 2010 due to poor growing conditions. This underlines how one bad weather season can lead to reduced supply and higher prices. But if ag has lagged in general, it might also hold the greatest opportunity of the three industries we've discussed. As I talked about in the last chapter, rising industrialization, higher standards of living and growing world populations are straining food supplies. This leaves farmers with the challenge of producing higher yields, particularly in light of urbanization and infrastructure development that is decreasing the amount of arable land. Potash is a proven yield enhancer and the most potash-intensive crops happen to be grains, which play a big role feeding people and livestock. Wheat, rice, corn and soybeans are part of the grain family; combined, these crops consume almost half of the world's potash.

The 2008 turmoil in financial markets led many of the world's farmers to suspend their potash purchases for a year, which took the price per tonne from about US$1,000 in 2008 to about $350.

Recent prices for potash have been rising and are expected to hover around $500 to $600 a ton by the end of 2010. Tellingly, new pricing contracts are for one year only. Potash Corp. has said it will agree to nothing longer than that, knowing the demand/supply dynamic behind potash. They also have one eye on the price of oil. Agricultural commodities—particularly potash— are highly sensitive to oil, so they're taking a strategic approach knowing higher oil prices may have to be factored into the price of potash in the days to come.

The bottom line is that farmers need fertilizer to maximize crop outputs and thereby ensure adequate grain production. Brazil's soybean growing land has increased 60% since 2000 due to its primary role meeting Chinese demand for the legume. India relies on potash for wheat and rice production and, as you know, there is little room for acreage growth, so higher yields are of paramount importance. Corn is another potash-intensive crop and demand will continue to grow due to livestock and ethanol requirements in fuel.

Whether it's gold, oil or agricultural commodities, the financial crisis has helped position these sectors for increased growth above and beyond what I expected pre-crisis. I talked about near-zero interest rates, budget deficits, and spending packages flowing like gasoline to the burning truck. What happens when it explodes? We're going to find out sometime over the next 10 years. To me, a boom is defined as a market with the right conditions to get carried away and deliver returns above normal. During a boom, people get excited about an asset class, and when they do, they throw money at it, and when they throw money at it, it goes up beyond what it would go up to on a long-term basis. The three industries we are discussing meet these conditions and are huge parts of the Canadian stock market. So that's really the connection. If you add up agriculture, gold and oil in Canada you get to a huge chunk of the Canadian market that is probably north of 47% and that's why you can come up with the statement of boom and rapid growth. That's when we'll see the real top of the boom. It will deliver the last 10%-to-20% overbought exuberance taking the S&P/TSX to 30,000.

The next step is profiting from it. And that's where we go next.

PART TWO

How to Profit from It

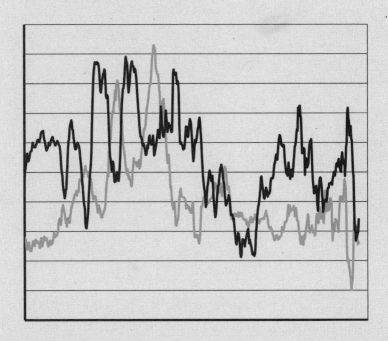

CHAPTER SIX

Buy stocks. Canadian stocks

"There's no place like home."
DOROTHY IN L. FRANK BAUM'S *THE WONDERFUL WIZARD OF OZ*

If you want to take advantage of the boom, you're going to have to buy stocks. Canadian stocks. There are a number of ways to do that, but before I share them with you, allow me to demonstrate through a single story the importance of buying stock. And then I'll finish up the chapter explaining why it makes sense to buy Canadian.

One important aspect of my job as CIO was to ensure Team Canada portfolio managers and analysts regularly met to review stock holdings. We took apart portfolios, assessing the merit of each company we were invested in to see if we would build the same portfolio today as we did yesterday. When I went to work for Peter Lynch after he'd hired me out of business school, one of the things that amazed me was the way every day he would approach each holding as a blank slate. Lynch had these yellow pads of paper he would carry to company meetings on which he would take notes. I remember attending two meetings with him. At the first, Lynch recorded everything the execs said and the responses to his questions. Shortly thereafter, the same guys would come back and Lynch started from scratch as if he never heard the story before. He asked the exact same questions, in the same order and jotted down everything over again.

He wanted to hear the story again, analyze it again and determine, as if he'd heard the story for the first time, whether he should invest in the company. Although I'm sure he had biases, he went into that second meeting driving the ball right down the middle of the fairway, asking the same questions, nodding the same way, scribbling down notes. He would do that every month, every quarter with every company he held or was thinking of holding in his portfolio. Each time he wanted to start from scratch. That was the goal during our Team Canada meetings: disassemble every portfolio to see if we would reassemble it the same way. The best way to do that is by constantly talking with companies and comparing your notes with others at portfolio manager meetings. You go to meetings, in a lot of cases, armed with knowledge or a thesis that you want to test with the next company that comes up for discussion.

At one meeting in 2003 a rookie analyst hired straight from McGill University introduced the team to a company in the paper and forestry sector. He had been researching the company for a couple of months and was a brave individual to be tabling anything in paper and forestry as it had been on the outs for some time. With the advent of email, people were using less copy paper while newspapers, magazines and the publishing world in general were migrating to the web. At the same time, lumber had become commoditized and sawmills across North America were hugely inefficient.

Veteran portfolio managers viewed the sector with skepticism but even in light of this bias, they could be persuaded by an analyst if the research was there to support the thesis. The company he spoke of was Sino-Forest Corporation. Although headquartered in Toronto, it grows and harvests trees in China and has a complementary engineered-wood products business. The company began in 1994 with an eye to capitalizing on China's growth prospects, particularly in home building. The analyst explained how Sino-Forest had leased large amounts of land to plant, replant and cultivate trees for harvest. He had made the trip to China, visited the plantations and met with company management in Hong Kong and Toronto. In 2003, the company had revenue of about $266 million, $30 million in net income and was trading for about $2 a share.

I liked the way the bottom-up fundamentals fit the top-down boom mosaic that was slowly coming together piece by piece. This is an example of what looking at the market through a different prism can do for you. Many might have dismissed Sino-Forest because of the industry it inhabits, but Sino-Forest was an example of a great stock idea lurking out there in an industry related to the boom. By 2007, the stock—in this terrible industry—had gone up to over $20 a share.

More broadly, the story illustrates the profit potential behind stocks. You can't get returns such as this from a bond or a GIC. In fact, there is no other play short of a lottery that holds out this wealth-building potential, which is why I believe you have to buy stocks. What does buying stock look like?

You can get your equity exposure in one of five ways: individual stocks, mutual funds, index, exchange-traded funds (ETFs) and hedge funds. I'll get into the pros and cons that come with each investment type. Then I'll explain why I think Canadian stocks offer the least risk and highest profit potential if you want to take advantage of the boom. One last word before we get into the details. In the next chapter I spend a lot of time talking about people who may want to do their own investing (buying stocks, picking mutual funds, for example). So I'm assuming the exact opposite in this one: that you're going to delegate the task of portfolio creation to someone else, be it an advisor or broker.

If you decide to go the route of doing your own investing, there is one thing to keep in mind: diversification. Yes, I talk about the brightest sectors being gold, oil and agriculture, but that doesn't mean you invest in these three areas alone. You're going to need some financials, some materials, consumer discretionary and so on. This is a lesson some of the best investors forgot during the tech boom.

I remember doing a broker dinner with another portfolio manager at a Toronto restaurant when there was still plenty of air left in the tech bubble. The two of us would present for an hour and then take questions. There were about 50 to 100 brokers in attendance and they were the best, smartest clients. It must have been the late fall of 1999 or winter of 2000. We were talking our normal shtick and I was basically outlining the early elements of this book. Not this thesis exactly—it was still forming, still an incomplete mosaic—but the overall attractiveness of commodities was something I was urging advisors to consider. Further, the sky-high valuations in tech were sending a clear message. I still owned tech at the time, but was downplaying the riskier, more aggressive companies saying, "It's very rare in the history of any developed market that a single stock gets to be of a size that it composes more than a third of the entire index, and I think there's a message in that. We really don't want anything like that kind of exposure after such a big run-up."

It's not to say I was picking that day as the top of the boom (we didn't reach the top, as measured by the tech-heavy NASDAQ stock index, until March 10), but at the time I thought less tech was better than more. Because of that, our funds were doing okay, but we probably weren't on top of the heap, because the winners in the fourth quarter 2000 were those that had abandoned reason and didn't diversify. They put all their marbles into an ever-declining number of incredibly priced and, as it turned out, overbought stocks. We were being the fuddy-duddies: we had tech, but we just didn't have that much and we didn't have the big names.

After the presentations at a broker dinner, it's a free-for-all in terms of questions. While a lot of advisors were asking intelligent, thoughtful questions, I remember one guy who simply wanted to tell me about his stock pick of the week and why it was going to be so good. He came up to me and said, "I don't invest my clients' money in mutual funds anymore because I can get more tech through a Canadian ETF." At that point, that would have meant the S&P TSX 60, which is more highly concentrated than an index fund. The reason he said he didn't invest in funds lay in the law that limits your exposure to 10% of any one name. That's a Canadian law: no one security can be more than 10% of your overall portfolio. So even though Nortel was roughly 40% of the ETF this guy was talking about, no mutual fund could hold more than 10% at what was called an at-a-cost basis. So if it went up, you could hold onto appreciation, but once you were past 10%, you couldn't buy any additional shares.

I told this guy, "Well, we don't have anywhere near the 40%. We're not going to tell you exactly what we have, but we don't think it's prudent to even use that ETF as a benchmark. If anything, we would look at something called a capped index where the limit is 10%, and we don't even have that much in Nortel." That's all we would say. In fact, we had quite a bit less than 10% at that point, but we don't like to tell people the specifics. But this guy came up with his scheme and told us, "I've gotten out of the mutual funds because they're limited to 10% and I've moved into this ETF where Nortel is 64% of the index." What he was doing for himself and his clients was feigning diversification by saying, "I'm getting you into an index," but in reality it was two-thirds Nortel.

I mentioned to him, "You're not diversified. You might as well just buy Nortel. You're just fooling yourself," and he kind of laughed at me. I never knew his name and I don't know what happened to him, but I hope he adjusted his strategy and got out in time. But it struck me that even professionals can get caught up in the moment and completely forget about diversification. I fell into that trap once.

I bought Homestake Mining in 1980, when I was a senior at school. It was the only stock I held at the time, but I knew I was a genius. I knew I would make a ton of money. I figured I was going to triple my investment in a few days. No real research, no real thought. Pure speculation.

The Hunt brothers were trying to corner the silver market, accumulate all of it and Homestake was a play off that because they mined silver. The Hunts drove the price of silver from US$11 an ounce in September 1979 to

US$60 an ounce by January 1980. That's when I bought it. Two months later, silver was below $11. The Hunts lost over a billion dollars. Then they were found guilty of conspiracy. They declared bankruptcy. Little Bob Haber thought he was going to ride along and make a mint, but I got killed. It wasn't a lot of money—I had around US$800 invested or something like that—but I was a kid, and it hurt. That was definitely a lesson learned.

I totally screwed it up and the reasons lay in a lack of diversification and research. How many other ways do I want to chastise myself? I was a regular odd lotter. I read about Homestake in the paper and by that time it was basically done. I piled in and learned my lesson the hard way.

It doesn't matter how smart you think you are. If you don't diversify, it never ends well. Diversification allows for margins of error. Not every stock is going to work out. You need to be diversified enough to allow for mistakes, which means a minimum of 30 stocks. The challenge for individual investors is that it's costly to buy a basket of 30 stocks with meaningful positions and then pay to adjust it over the years. Although trading costs have dropped considerably, you're still looking at about $500 to $600 to create a portfolio through your advisor or broker. Annual fees are another consideration, because you will trade them—not every day, sometimes not for months, but any good advisor is going to want to rebalance between good and better ideas once a year. In some instances, your advisor will knock out the stocks that didn't work and replace them with stocks that have better potential. So plan on average trading fees of about $200 to $300 a year.

As expensive as stock ownership may be, there are some positives worth mentioning. One of them is dividends, assuming you have dividend-paying companies in your basket. Getting a quarterly cheque is a nice thing. Further, your capital gains—the amount you enjoy if the stock rises and you sell—are preferentially taxed, so more of your profits stay in your pocket. Finally, many stocks have what are called dividend reinvestment programs (or DRIPs). DRIPs allow you to automatically reinvest your dividends in the stock you own by buying more shares instead of receiving a monthly cheque.

If stock ownership doesn't appeal to you, mutual funds are a great alternative. There are two kinds of funds to choose from: open-end and closed-end. I'll deal with open-end funds first because they are more familiar to investors and represent the majority of funds purchased in Canada and the United States. Open-end mutual funds pool the assets of investors and employ a professional money manager to make investment choices on behalf of the investment pool. Among the many positives associated with mutual funds, one of the biggest lies in the one-stop diversification you enjoy. As mentioned, it can be quite onerous and expensive to build your own portfolio with individual stocks, but with mutual funds you're able to gain exposure to 50, 100 or more stocks for as little as $1,000, or less if you choose an automatic investment plan. Further, you're able to hire a professional stock picker at a very reasonable cost: usually no more than 2.5% of the money you invest for equities and even less if you invest for bonds.

Closed-end funds share many traits of their open-end cousins: pooling the assets of many people, employing a professional to select investments and enjoying diversification at a low cost. The key differences between the two lie in the ways they're structured, purchased, sold and valued. Open-end mutual funds are structured so every new investor receives "units" in exchange for their money. The number of units issued is unlimited and they are purchased through the investment company offering them. Closed-end funds are purchased in the secondary market or from the stock exchange by a broker. And the number of units, or shares, is limited with just a few issued after the fund's launch, and rarely at that.

Because closed-end funds are traded on the open market, the value of each share of the fund will rise and fall—similar to an individual stock—throughout each trading day depending on market conditions and investor sentiment. Alternatively, open-end mutual funds are priced once a day at market close with their net asset value (NAV) determined by the total value of the individual securities in the fund divided by the number of units outstanding. This is where it gets interesting.

Because a closed-end fund's value is determined by

demand and supply in the market, the price attached to each share may be higher or lower than the daily NAV posted by an open-end fund. When the closed-end fund's shares are trading higher than the NAV it is said to be trading at a premium. When it's lower, it's said to be trading at a discount. To illustrate, if an open-end fund has 10 million units outstanding and the sum total of its portfolio holdings is $100 million, the NAV per share will be $10. But because closed-end funds are exchange-traded, the market value of its listed stock may be $1, $2 or $3 less than the NAV of the underlying portfolio. So in some instances, you could buy the same closed-end portfolio for $7, $8 or $9.

In March 2009 there were pages of closed-end funds listed in the paper trading at a 20% to 40% discount to the open-end versions. By buying at a discount, one can be positioned for potentially higher capital gains and higher dividend yield. Knowing you're buying a portfolio for less than the sum of its parts makes it pretty easy to stick your toe in the water. Over time, as the market comes to recognize the underlying value in a closed-end fund's portfolio, the discount narrows and may eventually move into the premium range, providing you with additional profits you wouldn't receive from an open-end fund. Further, the move into the premium range is a great indicator that the trade is over and it's time to take profits. In 1997 and 1998, Korea-focused closed-end funds traded at a deep discount to their open-end versions. By 2005–06, the closed-end funds had moved into a premium position so the opportunity to sell presented itself.

Looking at the bigger picture, the pricing of closed-end funds acts as a very good barometer of how the market feels. If you see closed-end funds selling at a discount, you can generally conclude that the market is feeling bearish. The opposite is true when you see them selling at a premium. So even if you're not going to invest in closed-end funds, they can play an important role as a market indicator. What's nice is that you can access pricing information and do quick comparisons between open- and closed-end funds at a variety of financial and business publication websites.

My final thought on closed- versus open-end mutual funds is to check who's managing the portfolio. If it's someone you're familiar with and trust and if they have a good long-term track record, that should seal the deal if you get a chance to purchase a closed-end fund at a discount.

If there is one drawback to closed-end funds, it's a lack of choice. In Canada, open-end funds outnumber closed-end ones by a long shot.

Alternatively, there is a wide range of open-end funds to satisfy just about anyone's investment needs. Stand-alone funds such as domestic, international and global equity; bond funds that invest here and around the world; balanced funds that bring the two together; and specialty and country-specific funds. You've got currency-hedged funds, U.S.-dollar denominated funds, inflation-protected funds, real estate funds and so on. In addition to stand-alone funds, there are fund of funds, which are portfolios built out of single-entity funds. These portfolios are constructed to cater to investors across the risk spectrum. And then there are target-date portfolios that adjust portfolio composition based on your investment time horizon.

There are many ways to take advantage of the boom through mutual funds. The way you choose will largely depend on number of years you choose to invest. Just ensure you have a good chunk of Canadian equity exposure. This could take the form of an all-equity domestic fund with U.S. and European equity exposure to aid diversification. Or maybe you add an energy or precious metals fund to spice it up. If you're a balanced fund investor, make sure it is a Canadian balanced fund. If you want a set-it-and-forget-it target-date plan, make sure it's got Canadian equity in it. You might end up with some other stuff in there, but you should at least explore this with your advisor to make sure you've got a solid position in Canadian equities. My final piece of advice on mutual funds is make sure you choose the right funds for you, and you don't want too many. Six to eight are ample. An alternate route, as mentioned, is to buy a pre-made portfolio. The key is to make sure you're buying one suited to your needs, the same way you would buy a van if you're a soccer mom and a Ferrari if you're single and 30 years old.

Index funds and ETFs are good alternatives to both open- and closed-end mutual funds. There are two notable differences between the two, otherwise they're near identical. Index funds and ETFs are priced once a day and are purchased through both a broker and an advisor. The latter can be traded any time of day as pricing is near real-time and you can purchase them only through a broker or an advisor with the appropriate license. Other than that, both are so-called "passive" investments, which means you're investing in a pre-determined set of stocks, unlike "active" investments where a portfolio manager picks and chooses. Whether you choose to go passive or active comes down to a single question: do you believe a portfolio manager can add value through research and find mispriced stocks as opposed to buying the whole market? It's a quantitative question. If you can get me an extra 2% or 3% a year in return, well, it's probably fair that I pay you half of one percent of that. You win, I win. But if you want me to pay a bunch and you can't beat the returns of an index or ETF, that's a bad proposition.

The big plus with both index and exchange-traded funds is pricing. They're both inexpensive. There's no living, breathing portfolio manager to pay. Because you're never going to do better than the overall market, you shouldn't pay a lot for the beta. (Beta is the market return whereas alpha is return above market.) A lot of funds don't beat the market, which means they don't give you any alpha. I ran a mutual fund company for 12 years and I can't dismiss that. And growth of 10% a year for 25 to 30 years is not a bad proposition, particularly with the added bonus of compounding.

The power of compounding is one of the miracles of life. You make money on money made. To illustrate its power, I noticed one example in a *Grant's Interest Rate Observer* newsletter dated November 27, 2009. The author used the example of Cleopatra, a lady who certainly understood the importance of power and money. If, as the newsletter stated, Cleopatra had invested $1 in 30 BC and it compounded annually at just 2%, it would be worth $343 quadrillion today. That's 6,000 times global GDP. It's a cheeky example, but it makes its point.

I'm not sure if Cleopatra would prefer index funds or ETFs over mutual funds, but there's no reason why you

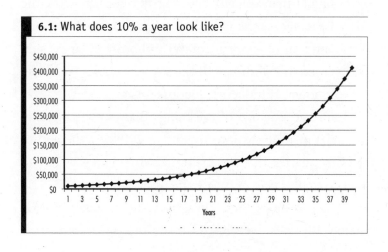

6.1: What does 10% a year look like?

can't mix them as well. This is called a satellite approach. You start with an index or ETF at the core and then add active management for sector and specialty funds. It's not a bad way to go. Just ensure, as I mentioned with mutual funds, that you've got exposure to Canadian equities. That could be an ETF or index fund that tracks the S&P/TSX, a U.S. fund that tracks the S&P 500 and a Canadian bond index fund with a couple of actively managed energy and gold funds. The combinations available to you are nearly identical to those in mutual funds.

Finally, there are hedge funds. I like hedge funds. The key to knowing whether hedge funds are right for you is the level of trust you have in the manager. If you really, and I mean *really*, trust the manager, you should be willing to give him the tools used by hedge funds to add value. Those tools are primarily short selling and leverage. Short selling involves borrowing a stock and selling it at a price higher than you will have to pay when you settle the loan. Leverage, as the word implies, is simply the use of a small amount of money (equity) to borrow a larger sum (debt) used to investment. If the strategy works, you make lots of money. If it doesn't, you lose lots of money.

Leverage was one of the things that got the big U.S. financial institutions into trouble in 2008. At the end of the first quarter, the leverage ratio at Lehman was 30.7 to 1, at Merrill it was 27.5 to 1 and at Morgan Stanley, 31.8 to 1. On average, these firms were borrowing approximately 30 times the value of its equity base and investing the proceeds. In comparison, the average leverage ratio for all U.S. commercial banks and savings institutions was 8.8 to 1.[1] It was also leverage, however, that delivered out-sized profits to Lehman, Merrill and Morgan Stanley's before 2008.

What got them into trouble was a lack of confidence and trust, a lack perhaps best exemplified with the fall of Bear Stearns. When Bear's institutional, hedge-fund and other top clients were no longer certain their money was safe, they demanded it back. So leverage can be a double-edged sword. Shorting is similarly risky. If, for instance, the stock you borrow (for a fee) doesn't fall in value but rises, you will have to "cover your shorts" by buying the stock at a higher price than what you borrowed it for with unlimited potential losses.

The attraction of hedge funds among traditional mutual fund managers is that during the hours of work managers expend finding the best investments, they also come across those they consider the worst. In the mutual fund world, the best you can do with that information is avoid the dogs. In the hedge fund world, you can put that knowledge to use by shorting, which may lead not only to greater profits but also to a lower risk profile for the fund as well. Like index funds, mutual funds and ETFs, there is a wide variety of hedge funds to choose from with many focused on Canadian equity. However, there are some drawbacks: hedge funds have high investment minimums, lower portfolio transparency and in many instances, you can withdraw your money only at pre-arranged times. Your advisor can help you determine whether a hedge fund is for you. Depending on your circumstances, you may want to mix hedge funds with both passive and active mutual funds.

I purposely did not include futures and options on my list of choices for equity exposure. I don't feel comfortable recommending them. The options and futures market creates no value—never has, never will—because it's a zero-sum game. You and I can both own a stock and we can make money "out of thin air." We can both become wealthy with no one becoming poor. But in the futures and options market, in order for us to become wealthy, someone has to become poor. There's a magic to owning equity because that's where the value is created, whereas in futures and options, you can win or lose a fraction of the pie, but the pie doesn't grow. I guess maybe that's the other way to put it. In equity, the pie can really grow.

Another area you want to avoid is trading soft commodities as opposed to hard commodities. *Soft* meaning wheat and corn in the agriculture sector, for example. *Hard* being things like oil and gold. Soft commodities are difficult to play by themselves because weather is such a huge part of their success. You can go from boom to bust in a year depending on temperature and rainfall. That really can't happen as often in oil or gold or any of the other hard commodities.

So let's get back to buying Canadian equities. I don't

Five reasons to buy stock. Canadian stock.

1. Stocks are the best way to build wealth over time.
2. You have a wide range of investment vehicles to choose from to develop a diversified portfolio.
3. Canadian stocks will leverage the boom.
4. Alternative propositions in Europe, the U.S. and the U.K. are low-growth by comparison.
5. Investing in Canada is low-risk compared to investing in China, Russia and other developing countries.

want to upset Canadians, but you've had this view in Canada for quite some time that the grass is greener everywhere else. Since 2005, Canadians have been cashing in their mutual funds that invest in Canada. I think that's a mistake. If Canadians continue to redeem, it's going to become a bigger mistake.

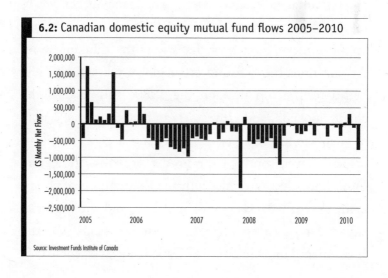

6.2: Canadian domestic equity mutual fund flows 2005–2010

Source: Investment Funds Institute of Canada

Canadians started to turn their backs on Canada in 2005 when the federal government scrapped the 30% foreign property rule, which obligated Canadians to invest at least 70% of their funds in Canadian assets. This finalized a process that started in 1971. Back then, Canadians were mandated by the government to have a minimum 90% of their funds in Canadian assets. That was lowered to 80% in 1994 and then 70% in 2001 before being eliminated four years later.[2] When the announcement was made it almost compelled people to take action, but looking back, it was a "be careful what you wish for" situation. Economists, industry analysts and commentators started beating the drum to get people to invest more outside Canada. They pointed out—correctly—that Canada represents only 3% of the world's stock market capitalization. Investing a high percentage of your total investable assets in Canada means you're missing out on much of the world's investment opportunities—or at least that's how the thinking went. At that time, the U.S. and other global markets had just had a terrific run through the 1980s and '90s, so the charts looked good. Investors and advisors took note of that strong prior performance, and a good chunk of money moved south of the border or across the ocean. Fund flows illustrate this, with the destinations of choice being global balanced funds and U.S. and international equity funds. At writing, the latest numbers from the Investment Funds Institute of Canada for 2009 show U.S.

equity holdings rising 19% with $3.9 billion added to the total. International equity was up 28% from the previous year with an identical $3.9 billion added. And global bond funds attracted $5.69 billion, while Canadian bond funds came second with $5.49 billion invested. Canadian equity was, on the other hand, the laggard compared to all three with $2.2 billion added to the category in 2009.[3]

And that's a shame. Canada was the star performer among major developed global markets from 2000 to 2009. Those markets include Japan, the U.S. and Europe. And when you measure Canada's performance against the broad MSCI World Index, the story gets better.

Alternatively, you know what's happened in U.S. markets over the past 10 years? Nothing. Looking forward, the economic picture is incredibly cloudy. Pick up and read the *Wall Street Journal* every day to track the discourse on the structural problems of unemployment, deficit and ballooning government. The U.S. has some pretty big obstacles to overcome in the coming years. I'm an American and I see it first-hand. The United States has competitiveness issues, it has unemployment problems, its housing prices continue to fall. Bankruptcies are on the rise, credit remains difficult to come by, there's a war on and we face monster budget deficits. The U.S. federal budget deficit for 2010 is predicted to come in at US$1.6 trillion according to the White House. By the end of the first half of fiscal 2010, the figure had been whittled down to US$1.3 trillion.[4] Who knows where it will actually wind up. If you were Aristotle in BC times and you spent $1 million a day every single day for 2,000 years, you still wouldn't get to the US$1.4 trillion mark.

According to the IMF's 2009 World Economic Outlook, the U.S. government debt to gross GDP is forecast to come in at 84.8% for 2009. For 2010, the estimated figure is 93.6% and for 2014, 108.2%. When public debt reaches a level that surpasses the equivalent of 90% of GDP, economic growth normally slows by 1% or more. Subtract that from the already anemic growth forecasts of about 3% for the U.S. and you're not left with much. This normally equates to lower returns on investment and financial assets. So I'm not sure the U.S. is where you want to be investing over the next five years. A similar story for Europe where Italy and Greece are both projected to exceed the 100% level in 2009, 2010 and 2014 in terms of debt to gross GDP. And in Britain, you've got an economy that's plagued by many of the same ills as the U.S.

Canada, as you know, sidestepped the housing debacle and the financial crisis, and is in a better position in terms of fiscal balance than most G7 countries. Canada's debt to gross GDP is forecast to be 78.2% in 2009 by the IMF and 79.3% for 2010. Britain, the world's fifth largest economy, may see its numbers jump to 98.3% by 2014 from less than 45% in pre-crisis 2007.[5]

These figures haven't been lost on a growing number of U.S. pension funds, hedge funds, endowments and sovereign wealth funds. SWFs in the Middle East, China and Russia are investing in Canada. These funds, which are owned and operated by governments, have traditionally been fuelled by profits coming from natural resources, particularly oil. Some of the better-known global SWFs are the China Investment Corp., the Kuwait Investment Authority and Temasek Holdings of Singapore. The province of Alberta has one called the Heritage Fund. SWFs may have as much as US$12 trillion worth of holdings by 2015.[6]

Aside from sheer size and investment clout, SWFs are important to Canada because they represent a shift in investment strategy over the past 10 years. Funds were once satisfied with a simple asset allocation strategy that, in the case of the SWFs, consisted of investing in lower-yielding bond assets. Now they're moving toward equity investments and "strategic asset" investments. Strategic investments are made for reasons above pure investment returns. The buyer usually has a bigger need to fill. In China's case, they're on the lookout for steel, oil, mining and, perhaps soon, fertilizer companies to ensure they guarantee themselves supply in the years ahead. When I think of all the world-class companies in Canada that have disappeared, it suggests to me that outsiders are buying because it's cheap and they see good growth prospects in a market that has been perpetually undervalued for years.

Going, going...

The following is but a partial list of the headline buyouts we've
seen where acquirers such as China, India, Russia and Brazil
have shown a long-term rather than speculative outlook. And
when buyers are thinking long-term rather than speculative, that
generally means that prices will be bid up.

2005
- Chinese state-owned China National Petroleum Corp. buys
  Calgary-based oil company PetroKazakhstan for $4.2 billion.

2006
- Arcelor, a European steel conglomerate, takes Hamilton-based
  steelmaker Dofasco for $5.6 billion. Arcelor subsequently
  merges with India's Mittal Steel to form ArcelorMittal.
- Brazilian mining giant Vale purchases Canadian nickel miner
  Inco for $15 billion.
- Switzerland-based miner Xstrata buys natural resource
  company Falconbridge, headquartered in Toronto, for $16.1
  billion.

2007
- Sault Ste. Marie's Algoma Steel falls to Essar Group, another
  major Indian steel producer, for $1.85 billion.
- Harris Steel Group sells itself to Nucor Corp., a Fortune 300
  steel company based in Charlotte, North Carolina, for $1.07
  billion.
- British-Australian mining group Rio Tinto purchases for $38
  billion the third largest aluminum producer, Montreal-based
  Alcan Inc., to become the world's largest aluminum company.

- Norilsk Nickel of Russia gobbles up LionOre Mining Ltd. for $6.4 billion to become the world's largest nickel producer.

2009
- Sinopec, the international arm of China Petroleum & Chemical Corp., purchases Calgary-based Addax Petroleum for $8.27 billion.
- Sovereign wealth fund China Investment Corp. buys into Vancouver mining company Teck Resources for $1.74 billion.
- PetroChina Co. purchases a $1.9 billion stake in Athabasca Oil Sands Corp.

2010
- PetroChina purchases a US$1.89 billion stake in Athabasca Oil Sands Corp.
- Sinopec buys a 9% stake in the Syncrude oil-sands project just outside Fort McMurray for US$4.6 billion.
- BHP Billiton Ltd. launches an unsolicited US$38.6 billion merger offer for Potash Corp. of Saskatchewan Inc.

Sources: *www.bloomberg.com, bbc.com, cbc.ca, theglobeandmail.com,* company reports

Not only are SWFs and others eyeing Canadian oil and commodities for strategic purposes, but investors outside Canada are starting to buy Canadian securities in record numbers.

According to StatsCan data, investors outside Canada acquired a net $10 billion of Canadian securities (stocks and bonds) in November 2009. At the time of writing, statistics for December 2009 are still forthcoming, but the November figure was was notable for being record-setting. In the year to date for 2009 investors outside Canada spent $97.8 billion on Canadian securities. This, as industry analysts pointed out, was part of the story behind the Toronto Stock Exchange's heady rise in 2009.[7] Interestingly, the bulk of the investments were in Canadian and provincial bonds. When bond guys give a country a thumbs up, it generally means the country they're endorsing is relatively stable. In other words, they think that country can repay its debts.

In addition to it having a solid economic foundation, Canada has the tailwinds of global industrialization at its back. To me this is a one-two knockout combination. I think in the coming years you'll see further pickup in investment flows to Canada as more strategic buyers recognize that Canadian stocks, bonds and companies are undervalued. This will further fuel the boom as people inside and outside the country begin to view Canada as a great investment opportunity. The prices of companies and the stocks they list will go up.

That's one of the reasons why your portfolio, no matter your style or risk profile, should have a lot of exposure to Canadian stocks. You may be wondering about the BRICs and the opportunities that may be had from investing in them through an index, ETF or mutual fund. Goldman Sachs being the leader in BRIC research has to do with the product offering they launched to coincide with the research release. The company launched a suite of country-specific funds and the research reminds you of that. This is where you have to confront the risk-reward equation.

The People's Republic of China (PRC), for all its free-market liberalization, is still a centrally controlled country that's rigidly run by the government with a limited track record when it comes to security law, investor rights and personal property.

Almost a third of the 70-page December 2009 prospectus for the BlackRock branded iShares FTSE/Xinhua A50 China Index ETF is devoted to the risks of investing in China. Among the risks mentioned: political changes, social instability and adverse diplomatic developments that could, as the prospectus states, "result in the imposition of additional restrictions including expropriation of assets, confiscatory taxes or nationalization of some or all of the property held by the underlying issuers of the A Shares in the index."

In plain language, what this caution means is that the PRC may, if it chooses, simply take control and ownership of companies. That's what happened in the Venezuelan oil sector when President Hugo Chavez nationalized the country's oil deposits by decree on May 1, 2007, saying he was taking over property and management of foreign-run oil deposits. This impacted many of the world's leading oil extractors, including BP, ExxonMobil, Chevron, ConocoPhillips, Total SA and Statoil. After nationalizing oil, Chavez turned his attention to the rigs that do the drilling, eventually taking over 11 of them, which were owned by American-run Helmerich and Payne.[8]

In addition to nationalization concerns, the legal and judiciary systems in most emerging countries are uncertain at best. In China, the Supreme People's Court, the ultimate arbitrator of its legal system, is based on written statutes (a good thing) but the court is free to interpret cases as it sees fit with prior decisions carrying no precedent value (a bad thing). Much has been done to bring Chinese commercial law into line with Western standards, but again, investing in China remains a bit of a dice roll because, as the prospectus states, Chinese commercial law is still "new," "experimental," and "evolving."

India rules itself by traditional British legal precepts and by parliamentary democracy, which puts it a big step ahead of the other BRIC countries. But at the company level, a great deal more work needs to done with regard to financial data, accounting and reporting standards. In Russia, financial information is opaque at best and invented at worst. Other general risks that come with investing in emerging markets include liquidity, currency movements, transparent market pricing and repatriation of funds.

This tells me two things about emerging market investing. It's inherently risky, and if you're going to dip your toe in these waters, you'll want an active manager taking care of your investments. The portion of my portfolio (5%) that I've invested in a stand-alone emerging market fund is managed by a living, breathing human being supported by plenty of analysts.

I think active management, particularly a market fundamentalist, adds value in emerging markets because a manager can interpret financial statements and reporting. A fund manager also has the opportunity to meet company management in person, which is a big plus. Seeing is believing. The amount of information we gleaned from face-to-face meetings with management was impressive. In many instances, what's revealing is not the answers senior executives give (all that is in the public realm already), but rather the tone of their voice, their gestures and the emphasis given to certain subjects.

As I said earlier, I respect index and exchange-traded funds, but the portfolios created through replication or representative sampling in emerging markets are awfully concentrated. For example, as at December 2009, the iShares China Index ETF has placed over 45% of its assets in the top 10 companies listed on the Shanghai and Shenzhen indexes and eight out of the 10 are financial services related—banks and insurance companies.

Concentration can lead to volatility. And no investment is worth it if you're going to cash in due to the huge swings in value. The BRICs have taken most of the investing spotlight and have delivered larger-than-life returns in some years. But in others, the losses were crushing. In 2007, for instance, the iShares China Index ETF delivered an eye-catching 135.71% one-year return. But in 2008, it fell 66.2% for the year and then sprung back in 2009, notching an 80% return. The big question is whether you have the stomach to endure such big performance swings.

I think it makes sense to maintain a big percentage of your portfolio in the developed world, meaning the G7. The numbers say we already do, as illustrated by the chart.

The point of this chapter is simple: if you want to participate in the boom, it's called Canada. And the best way to do it is buying stock.

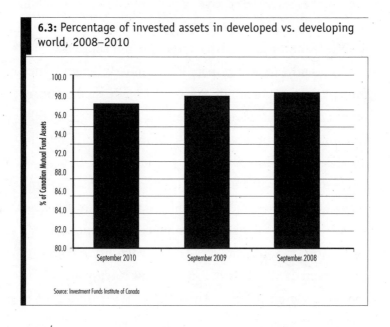

6.3: Percentage of invested assets in developed vs. developing world, 2008–2010

Source: Investment Funds Institute of Canada

CHAPTER SEVEN

Know thyself

"Knowing thyself is the beginning of all wisdom."
ARISTOTLE

By the summer of 2000 the team had grown to a decent size. We now numbered about a dozen analysts and portfolio managers. It was time to do a little team building and have some fun.

I decided on an offsite. The place I chose was the racetrack at Lime Rock Park in Lakeville, Connecticut. The track is about two or three hours from the Boston office, so I arranged for a bus to take us up the day before. This gave us a chance to spend Saturday afternoon working, have dinner and then race on the Sunday.

I didn't exactly tell the team what to expect at Lime Rock, but the track is well-known in racing circles. It opened in 1957 and hosts NASCAR, Grand-Am and ALMS events. The track is just over 1.5 miles long and has seven turns. In the stretch, cars can reach speeds above 125 mph. In other words, it's a bit scary.

To help us navigate the course or simply stay on it, we spent the morning in the Skip Barber driving school. There we learned emergency braking, turning at high speeds and what to do when you started to lose control. The cars we were driving were open-wheeled and looked like the Formula One race cars you see on TV.

After the morning's instruction, we had lunch and then headed back to our cars. Each of us was strapped in—they had to remove the steering wheel so my legs could fit—and the race was on. After a couple of laps, something interesting happened. I noticed some managers and analysts were out in front, zipping past two-thirds of the group. Other members of the group—mostly older— were, on the other hand, taking a slower, more measured approach as they whipped around the course.

On the way back to Boston that night, I started to think about the way each team member had managed the course. It struck me that the way they approached the track loosely correlated with their level of risk. Some of the guys were more comfortable taking on more risk in the corners and speeding through the straightaway. Others were somewhere in the middle: willing to take risk but not enough to spin out. The third group was slightly behind us in the risk-taking category.

As CIO, part of my job was assigning portfolio managers to funds. Knowing where each team member fell on the risk scale helped me determine which funds they were best suited to managing. In the coming years, I would think back to the day at Lime Rock as I created new products and asked team members to run them. I would draw a parallel to how they raced that day. During those discussions, team members would see similar parallels— they learned something about themselves. Steve Binder, a terrific investor, is one of the best in the business when it comes to investing in large companies. He is a cautious, value investor who focuses on the balance sheet. Very sharp. That doesn't mean he isn't willing to make big bets. In fact, he has made some very big bets. That's part of the reason that Lipper named Binder's fund—Fidelity True North—Fund of the Decade. But those bets were in an arena that lent itself to a value-oriented, balance sheet–centric investor. The funds he managed and the ones he assisted on were not, as you would expect, fast-trading, volatile investment products. Binder is better suited to patient, diligent, blue-chip investing. He knows this partly because of the day at the track.

Where would you fit on the racetrack? Are you a hard-driving risk-taker? Or a more steady, cautious investor? Knowing the answer is the central thesis to this chapter. This is particularly important if you're going to buy individual stocks to take advantage of the boom. Based on figures I've seen from Canadian discount brokerages, more of you are considering this option. I understand this. I think individual investors enjoy real advantages over the pros. You don't have to restrict yourself to one style (growth, value, blend) or market cap (small, medium, large). There is no sector, geographic or industry constraints. If you want to invest in gold, the U.S. or health care, you can go ahead and do that. And you don't have to keep a cash reserve available to meet redemptions, as the pros must, or concern yourself with investing large, new influxes of cash. There are no liquidity concerns, trading execution is straightforward and there are no daily reports, quarterly reviews or annual assessments. This may be the biggest plus. You can invest for the long term instead of managing for the quarter. No one is looking over your shoulder. Unless of course, it's your spouse.

As many advantages as there are to do-it-yourself stock-picking, it's important to know first whether you're up for it. I'm not sure enough people take a hard look in the mirror before they open an account, and learning as you go is not something I recommend when you've got retirement or a kid's college fund on the line. Building your investing self-awareness is what this chapter is about. Although the majority of my remarks are confined to stock-picking, there's plenty in here for mutual fund investors who stitch together portfolios of funds for themselves. Being self-aware as an investor means knowing your inclination to research, the manner with which you track and monitor stocks, your reactions to setbacks and your propensity to buy when others aren't. Remember 2008? It was a generational buying opportunity, but a lot of people sold. Did you? Your answer will say a lot about you. These are some of the things I'll cover in the following pages. If I'm at all successful, you'll be in a better position to decide whether you should be doing the stock-picking and investing or leaving it to someone else.

When I got the job as CIO in 1997, the first thing I needed to do was build a team. To cover virtually every stock in the Canadian marketplace, which is what I felt we needed to do, I needed enough analysts and portfolio managers to do the job. So I needed to start hiring. And from day one, I knew I wanted Canadians because I really wanted this to be a bona fide Team Canada. I wanted people who would take pride of ownership from the fact that their family, relatives and friends may have invested in the funds they managed. I went about hiring in two ways: directly recruiting from top business schools at Canadian universities and searching top U.S. business schools for Canadian students.

This made the recruitment job tougher. My potential recruits were needles in the haystack. Not only were we looking for Canadians, but we had to find Canadians who were also willing to live in Boston—away from their families and loved ones—for an extended period of time. How long, none of us were really sure. My long-term plan was to bring them back to Canada one day, but it would have been silly to promise that upfront or provide a hint of a timeline. So here I was laying down some pretty rigorous criteria to find people.

But if my recruiting job was tough, I think it was even tougher for the people wanting to get hired. I've said Team Canada is one of the toughest teams to join. That's no overstatement. You have to be at the top of your class and your area of study or the best at your job, but not only that: the reason why you are the tops and the best has to be because you want to do the job—because you love it. Love the fast pace. Love the pressure. And more than anything else, love the activities associated with buying stocks. It can't be about the money or the word "Fidelity" on the business card. It has to be about the stocks.

Every spring starting in 1997 we'd hit McGill, the University of Toronto and Queen's, among other schools, to conduct interviews. Fidelity still goes back today and the list of schools has expanded. The number one prerequisite is for the candidate to love stocks, and I mean really love them. So I looked for people who as kids joined clubs to buy and sell stock. People who read up on stocks like some read up on celebrities. People who loved spending their evenings reviewing stock tables, company reports and the business pages. People who looked forward to receiving stock shares for Christmas or on their birthday, so they could follow a new company the rest of the year and attend the annual meeting.

I remember one hire who, when we tracked him down, had stacks of annual reports piled in the living room of his college apartment in Montreal. When I asked him what he did with them, he told me flatly, "I enjoy reading them."

He got hired. And he has proven himself to be a top fund manager. He's a hard worker and wants to learn about companies, their management teams, the business engines behind their growth and their fundamentals. One of the keys to his success is the fact that he loves doing what he's doing. You should look to yourself for a similar passion because investing, particularly stock-picking, can eat up a lot of your day. I would say most people in the business view it as a passion as much as it is their work.

Remember my cottage I spoke about at the start of the book? Over the winter holidays my family holes up there for a couple of days. In early January, we had gifts to bring back to the store for exchange so we went to a local mall. Due to its rural location it's a relatively small mall but there are some familiar stores, among them, Best Buy, Victoria's Secret, The Children's Place and Claire's. I've never been big on retail investing but every time I saw one of these stores the ticker symbol flashed through my head: BBY, VS , PLCE and CLE (as they were known at the time). Although I didn't go into each store, I made a point of looking to see how well-kept and well-lit it was and how much traffic was moving through it. Basically I was wondering if it was a happening place and whether the stock price reflected that. I couldn't help myself. It wasn't a stressful thing. It's just something that's always on my mind. I'm sure the same thing happens to a train hobbyist when a locomotive comes rumbling down the track.

Look for cues in your behavior. Do you read market updates, follow company news and digest earnings reports? If, after some introspection, you find you really are captivated by the markets, what moves them and the companies that populate the investing universe, you probably have the right makings for a stock-picker.

The next thing to get a handle on is your investor type. What stocks are you drawn to? What do you like to research? What are your strengths and weaknesses when it comes to investing? What is your risk tolerance? We touched on these questions a bit at the start of this chapter, but because they are central to knowing yourself as an investor, let's revisit them from a couple additional angles. I'll start with the risk aspect and then broaden it out to the other areas.

To some people, risk is the potential for loss. For others, it describes the level of volatility. I think it's a bit of both. I don't think there's any real way to understand how much volatility you're able to withstand until you've lived through it. I'm starting to see investment management companies and banks come out with practice trading accounts. These give you a fictional amount of money, say $100,000, and you can buy and sell to your heart's content. This is good in theory. But like a schoolyard bet between youngsters who don't intend to exchange money regardless of the outcome, it's a step away from reality. Until you've put your money down, until you have skin in the game, you won't know for sure where you fall on the risk spectrum. As much as I thought I knew a new portfolio manager's risk comfort level, I would never know for sure until I watched that manager invest money for a period of time.

So with Steve Binder, the balance sheet guy I told you about earlier in the chapter, I was eager to pull him out of research where he worked as an analyst and promote him to portfolio manager. For a long period, he was a top-performing analyst based on his stock recommendations, so I felt he was ready. I thought his patient, diligent makeup was particularly well-suited to manage the equity component of a balanced fund. We didn't have a balanced fund in Canada though I thought it would make a great investment product. I was the original portfolio manager on the U.S. Fidelity Balanced Fund launched for American investors in 1986, which had grown to over US$5 billion in assets 10 years later. It was a great success for both investors and the company and I thought a Canadian version would be equally well-received, but before I introduced it—or any investment fund in Canada—I wanted to make sure I first had the expertise to manage it. Knowing yourself can also apply to the company you work at. And knowing ourselves meant knowing when you had the appropriate people in place to manage particular funds. I thought Binder was the guy for the equity portion of the balanced fund, but I made sure not to throw him in right away. Until you see people with money on the line, until you see their investment process in action and the types of stocks they're drawn to, you're not really sure about their risk profile. So I would give prospective managers initial assignments and little sums of money to manage to help me determine their profiles. That's what I did with Binder.

Along the way, you find out other things about a

person's investor type. All of us have strengths and weaknesses when it comes to investing and it pays to know what you are good at and what you're not so good at. After you've determined a person's investor type, the next step is to get managers to buy into their own strengths, to reward them for their strengths, to make sure they're happy and satisfied sticking to what they do best rather than feeling they have to do everything, or wanting to do every little thing. That's the process we worked through in developing Team Canada where we would have an analyst cover just 14 stocks or thereabouts.

That may seem restrictive, but not everyone can run, in the Fidelity context, the True North Fund. That's the flagship fund that Binder ran for many years after he proved himself on the Fidelity Balanced Fund, which debuted in 1998. But you need a different type of investor to run an income trust portfolio or a special situations portfolio. The key is knowing the people you've worked with, to convince them that you know them and, together, for you to come to a decision that this where that person going to do best because you've done real time work together understanding that person's strengths and weaknesses.

A key to building a strong balanced fund is having people who excel at their specialties manage individual components. One is good at large-cap equities, another small caps and then another high-yield bonds and still another government and investment-grade bonds.

Without them doing their bit and being motivated, the balanced fund or the asset allocation fund wouldn't be nearly as good. Taken together, the whole is going to be special and the record proves it: it is special.

But along the way, you also have to convince these people that they can't do some other things. You don't want them to do those other things, because you want them to get really great at investing in small companies or in some sector or in bonds. I think that specialization is the difference between winning or losing at the end of the day and that's something individual investors should make note of. Some people think they can invest in anything and be a success. This confidence might just be part of their character, or it might come down to their maturity level. Sometimes people just say "No, I'm going to be a star. I can be the star whatever I choose to invest in."

As the bio on the flap of this book notes, in 2002 I became a part owner of the Boston Celtics basketball team. I once asked Celtics coach Doc Rivers about individual strengths and weaknesses and how he manages to bring them all together as a team. Doc, who who is a two-time winner of the NBA Coach of the Year, is great at this. He builds a team out of guys who for their whole lives have been the best player on the team. Doc has to get each player to buy into the player's individual strengths and weaknesses, and he has to use that player's strengths and weaknesses as motivation. The things that player does well can be important to the team and to the player personally. It's Doc's job to get them to focus on that stuff.

I spoke with Doc at the Celtics practice facility in Waltham, a suburb outside Boston. Other than the game days, that's where you find the team, the coaches and trainers because we don't own the arena. The practice facility is world-class in its own right with a state-of-the-art gym, full-size NBA basketball court and custom-sized locker and dressing rooms. The Celtics have won the most championships in the NBA and the original banners hang over the court at the facility. They're a bit ragged, yellow with age and it looks like someone spilled coffee on most of them. The starched, clean championship banners you see on TV at the Garden are replicas. I go out to the facility every once in a while to observe practice. It's fun. Practice is a different side of the game.

Doc says it's a real challenge to get players to recognize their individual strengths, focus on them and play to them. The key is to share the data or stats you're using to make your decision, convince them you're doing what's right and to accentuate the positive. You don't say, "You can't shoot" he told me. What you do say is, "You're the best rebounder we have, so we need to place you away more often from your shooting position, so you get the rebounds." You want to accentuate the positives, because you've got them on the team for some positive reason, and if you don't, then you ought to get rid of them.

It's brutal if you play to your weakness in the NBA. We have a guard who's now an all-star. His name is Rajon Rondo. What an athlete. Spectacular. But he doesn't happen to be a great outside shooter. He's really developed all the other skills, but the rest of the league, when it gets to crunch time, wants to force him to shoot from the outside. It's brutal. They set up their whole defence so he is forced to shoot from the outside. Now if he said to himself, "Screw you, I'm taking on this challenge and I'm going to do it, I'm going to shoot it each and every time," that would hurt the team quite a bit.

So he'll hold onto the ball and try to pass it. And the reason he's doing that isn't because Doc said, "Don't shoot," it's because he knows when he should shoot to maximize—though it's a hard thing to say. It's easy for someone like Rondo, who's among the best, to say, "I'm going to do this. You can't leave me open. Screw you. I'm shooting it." But that would diminish the team's efficiency. The same would be true in our business if a quantitative manager suddenly decided, for example, to take a fundamentalist approach to investing. Predicting the future is more fun than running a bunch of algorithms on the past, right? That's obvious. But regardless of how alluring fundamental investing may be, the quantitative manager would be playing to his weakness.

And if guys play to their weakness when investing, it's brutal. You'll get killed. Peter Lynch, one of the greatest mutual fund managers of all time, rarely, if ever, strayed out of his areas of expertise. Warren Buffett is exactly the same way. You don't see Buffett investing in technology companies. He tells you, "I don't understand them." So he owns prosaic companies. Railroads, soft drinks, gum and insurance companies. The smartest investors are always playing to their strengths.

If all of a sudden Buffett decided to invest in companies he didn't understand—"Well, heck. I'm the richest guy in the world, the best investor maybe ever. I'm going to buy some technology companies just because I can. I'll be right because I'm blessed with some fairy dust"—he'd be playing to his weakness and he would probably get stomped on pretty good even though he's Warren Buffett.

My first piece of advice to investors who want to buy stocks and build their own portfolios is to start with a small amount of money and find out what you're good at, what you like to invest in, how much risk you can take. You've got to figure out where you can best succeed. That was a big part of my job: trying to make sure for the sake of the person and the organization that I placed people in roles where they could succeed.

That's where you want to be as an individual investor, but it takes time. You won't really know your risk tolerance until you've done this for a bit and with real money. You can always move up the ladder. Pay particular attention if you're down 20%, 30% or 40%. How do you respond? In 2008, most people were down by this much whether it was a stock, an equity mutual fund or a portfolio. It was a real testing ground for a lot of people. If you weren't sleeping and you were tearing your hair out, you had probably exceeded your risk threshold. If, on the other hand, you said, "buying opportunity, very rare," you may be less risk-averse and you may want to dial up your risk profile a bit.

For me, the top of the risk scale is someone who owns a couple of stocks—one, two or three—all residing in the same industry category. In other words, the basket is too small and it's undiversified. That's way too risky but it is there, way out there on the risk spectrum. I sometimes wonder how many people live in this neighbourhood. The next level down is a diversified basket of stocks, say 30. Introducing a bond or fixed-income component to the basket of stocks or investing in a combination of bond and stock mutual funds takes you another step down the risk meter. To further reduce the risk profile of the investment portfolio, you simply increase the allocation to bonds and reduce the allocation to stocks. If you're looking for even less risk, at some point you'll start introducing cash equivalents into the mix or a money market fund until your equity exposure or stock holdings represent a small percentage of overall assets. So there's a broad spectrum of risk and somehow you have to place yourself somewhere on it.

Age also enters the equation here. In addition to noticing the linkage between team members' levels of risk and how they handled the track, I couldn't help thinking that there was another factor at play: age. The younger the drivers, the more daring they were. It may be okay to jump off the track and hit the hay bale when you're 22 or 23, but at my age, it wasn't something I was prepared to do. Obviously, if you're 70 you simply don't have enough time to make up for losses, so your risk tolerance drops. If you're 25 and you're investing for when you're 70, you'd be willing to take a loss, which allows you to dial up the risk.

A final thought on risk. When the markets cratered in 2008, I had a lot of conversations with the press, who wanted to know why I wasn't selling everything. "Just go to cash" was the directive. Well, from my point of view, when the market falls 700 points in a day or, as it turned out, 4,500 points in a couple of months, most of the risk was taken out of the market. When the S&P/TSX is at 14,000 points there is more risk than when it's at its bottom. In 2000, you could smell the risk in the air like propane off a still-unlit barbeque. That's why I take pains in the last chapter of this book to identify the signs associated with the market reaching its top. The boom will froth near the end and there will be a time to rebalance your investments to compensate for the additional risk. But there will also be opportunities as the boom gathers force to buy on dips, or corrections. As I've stated, the path the boom takes will not be straight up. Experienced investors understand this and are ready to take advantage of it.

Are you?

That's a question you want to be able to answer, because buying dips, buying declines, buying weakness is a really smart thing to do. Unfortunately, it's also one of the toughest things to do. It's hard because psychology is a huge element of the business. But unless the world has turned upside down, people should be buying 10% and 20% corrections. If you look back at the history of market declines, the common trait among investors is to sell their investments, be it equity mutual funds, stocks, whatever. They liquidate their positions. That's when you've got to zig instead of zag. That's why I point to that one chart that people should fix in their minds when the market is way oversold. The chart has never been wrong. The market has always come back and righted itself over time. If you know from previous corrections that you're a seller, it may be best to find someone to do the buying for you. Finding that level of self-awareness will make you a better investor because there will be dips along the way to the boom. Taking advantage of those dips will be important to profiting from the boom.

The next thing to ask yourself if you want to be a do-it-yourself investor and stock-picker is whether you want to spend the time on research. Generally, if you aren't interested in the research process or you're unable to find the time to do it, you're going to be in trouble on individual stocks.

On a lark my sister sent me a subscription to the *Wall Street Journal* when I was in college. I think it was 1975. I was the only one in my college frat house who received it. The rest of the guys thought I was a weirdo. And I've read it every day ever since. In addition to reading the *Journal* daily, I read the *New York Times*, the online edition of the *Globe and Mail*, and a clutch of e-newsletters and market opinion stuff that arrives by email. Weekly, I'll read *Barron's* and *Forbes* magazine and have a couple of books—fiction and non-fiction business—going as well. I may spend up to 10 hours a day reading with 75% of the time devoted to market-related material. I'm not even working full-time so I don't see half the work-related research I used to. I am, I think, fairly representative of most good portfolio managers who spend as much time— or more—as I do reading. But they gravitate to different material than I do. That's worthy of note because each investor will be interested in something a little different. Their choice of subject matter says a lot about the type of investor they are, the things they choose to invest in and how they invest.

I've known some who read obscure trade magazines to find subtle changes in industries. Is a company coming out with a new product? Have they found a way to innovate a process? Is there a new threat to a particular business? What these managers look for are incremental changes that may impact a company or industry. Changes that aren't worthy of attention in mainstream papers, magazines and television. By staying current with seldom-followed but cutting-edge trade magazines, these managers are getting ahead of the curve and hoping to exploit potential top-line growth, which tends to be small and at early stages of development, in the companies they track.

Contrast that with Binder, who chooses to devote more time to annual reports and balance sheets of larger, more established companies. Binder is, in fact, so enamoured with balance sheets he created a model of the Massachusetts state budget in his spare time. This was while he was managing money. He would update the model quarterly, inputting tax revenues, disbursements and expenditures to see if he could predict where the budget was headed in terms of a deficit or surplus. And then he would monitor the numbers to see what was on course and what was off. If that's what he did as a hobby, I said to myself at the time, I can only imagine what he's doing with the companies he owned.

You should go with the flow. If you find yourself reading about large, big-cap companies, it doesn't make sense for you to be trading penny stocks. And the reverse is true.

I like to read macro-type stuff, and I have an eye out for anything that's statistically anomalous. Information that sticks out. If you ask me what I thought about IBM's earnings or something like that I'd be clueless, because it just doesn't stick to me. Reading the bigger picture stuff and keeping an eye out for incongruities and anomalies helps me identify what I call "key" moments.

Let me illustrate what I mean by a key moment using the 2008 market crash as an example. The lead-up to it and the period after yielded two key moments. The first was when I noticed widening credit spreads. That stuck out to me as a key moment to make substantive allocation changes to our products. Identifying the moment was the first step. Acting on it was the second. The other key moment emerged after the big damage had been inflicted on the markets.

Everyone was trying to discern a bottom—a difficult task. When the market is heading towards the bottom, I can tell you that very few people are able to look at their watch and say, "Aha! I've got to get in at this moment." I don't work that way. I work through a process where I look for things that diverge from the norm. So in March, every bit of bad financial news was met with more selling. Day after day, week after week. But by May, the bad news was no longer met by violent waves of selling. That stuck out to me. For me, that was the bottom, the key moment. I started buying. I think acting in this way is different than market timing because it's the result of a different process. Because I wasn't just buying and hoping for the best. I was buying because I'd seen something— something different—and then I overlaid a process that lead to an action.

Key moments are relatively rare because the market generally moves sideways: up slightly, down slightly with no great event pushing it one way or another. You wouldn't gather this from reading the papers or watching TV, where there's always somebody wringing their hands or flailing like a chicken, but on the whole, the markets usually move between shades of normal. It's only once in a while that a key moment comes along. It could be a key moment for the market as a whole, or it could be a key moment for an industry or even just one company. But at these key moments you have to dig in and take advantage. In some instances, you can see key moments building.

I was attracted to the Federal Reserve as subject matter for the class I'm teaching at Tufts is because I think we're closing in on a key moment in fiscal and monetary policies. I have no formal training on the Fed, nor did I ever work there or study it specifically in school. I'm training myself as an expert on the Federal Reserve because I think it's going to be important.

As the U.S. tries to figure its way out of the mess it got into to save itself from depression, we're being set up for a key moment or maybe a couple of key moments. The Fed's going to have a monster role in the economy in the coming years. What's that going to mean for interest rates, stocks and the economy? Along the way, something will stick out as unusual or different, and when that point comes, you have to be willing to do the research, apply your buy-and-sell process and take advantage of the moment. That's how a multi-faceted research approach differs from market timing. We've talked about gold, oil and ag, and I own those personally. I have significant positions in these areas and I think you should have exposure to them for the next several years. But there will also be some key moments around them. Oil may, for instance, drop a lot due to one thing or another. When that happens, I will remind myself of my long-term thesis—oil is going to boom—and I will buy more at that point because I'll recognize this is a key moment. The same for gold. And ag.

So if you're going to be a stock-picker, I think you've got to be a reader and a researcher, and you've got to recognize the information you're drawn to as a reader. Everyone will be different. Everyone's interests are different. That's what it means to know yourself.

Another important thing to know about yourself is your need for control. At most large investment management firms, the portfolio managers and analysts have four or five screens at their work stations. One or two of them display what are called heat maps. On any given day, you look at your portfolios—personal, professional, considered— and the heat map will show you in red and green what's getting killed and what's doing great. It changes every second. It's the same thing if you're an individual investor and you follow your portfolio second by second on your discount brokerage account, or you follow the daily NAVs posted alongside your mutual funds.

These heat maps are the worst. Everyone's got them now, but I think they were the worst invention. I think others do too. It's instantaneous, but it's irrelevant. It means worrying about something you have no control over. Another example would be watching CNBC or BNN in Canada and fretting about each new opinion or, even worse, changing your investment thesis each day. You can consume hour after hour watching this stuff and looking at heat maps and it will provide nothing in return. There's no forward value in it.

Further, when I was managing money, I never looked at results until the end of the quarter or when I had to. There are a lot of sports analogies here. People who watch the score after every point or second are taking their focus off the game. I think I was probably the oddball on this one, but I could not tell you how I was doing day to day and to the penny. I chose not to look because I couldn't think what good it was going to do me. As with the heat map, I don't think there's any value in being up to the minute. If you're a portfolio manager, you know in your bones whether your fund is doing well or not. I'm sure the same can be said for the average investor and their stock portfolio. You know when it's working and when it's not working, but wanting to know to the penny isn't productive to me. The other thing is that most of your clients don't care. For do-it-yourselfers, your client is probably your spouse. You should care about what they care about. They care if the quarters roll into years and the years roll into retirement. That's what they care about. And you have to remind yourself that you're investing for years, not for the second.

Something else investors need to keep in mind is that sometimes it isn't a manager's fault when stocks fall. The market has its own crazy moments. In 1990 I was managing money in the U.S. and I had invested in some great companies that were doing well, but the U.S. was embarking on the Gulf War and there was a recession. It didn't matter at that moment that my companies were doing well. They just got cheaper and cheaper. So you have moments in time when the market isn't controlled by what you're good at. You could be a good investor, understand your risk profile and do all the research, but at some moments, the market is influenced by technical or outside forces beyond your control.

If you're a fundamental guy in situations like this, you tend to feel like you don't know anything. You feel lost. You feel as if the knowledge you have is so irrelevant, you must be clueless. A big part of knowing yourself is understanding what you're going to do in situations like this. You should develop a plan, a process to deal with it. A lot of people who don't have a plan react to these situations by trading. Turning things over. Doing something to get the screen to turn green, or quiet the voices on TV, or squeeze out an extra penny on a stock— any stock—by the end of the day.

My solution is to look away, to turn it off. Get out of the office and speak to companies—the ones you are invested in—to remind yourself why you bought them in the first place, or to do research on the ones where you're thinking of investing. Your time is better spent this way. There's value in this activity. For the do-it-yourself fundamentalist, you might revisit the research that led you to invest in the company. Or you could ferret out more research, look for a different source perhaps or look at your research in a new light. You'd know you're doing something positive.

We took the same approach on the quant side, which relies on computer models to assist in filtering stocks, among other things. When things aren't going your way, don't fret or look at the screen. Instead, look inside your process, see if there was a cleverer way to decode the models or whatever filters you're using to find stocks. You should spend time on the things you *can* control. If you're a fundamentalist, call another company. If you're quant, retune a model or something else. If you're a technician who studies stock patterns, derive more charts. Whatever.

You can get caught up in quarterly reporting and daily trading. Newspapers have to tell you why the market went up or down yesterday, which is mostly irrelevant, so people end up reacting instead of thinking. Years ago, there was less information available and you had more time to process it.

When I was doing analytical work for Fidelity in 1985, we were working with the first personal computer. We're talking about the IBM PC. We were using something called Lotus. If you wanted to change a bunch of things in your financial models, you would hit "Enter" and go to lunch, and when you came back an hour later, the thing would spit out your new case. I actually think that was okay. That was a good time frame to work within. You were forced to think more about what went into the models. Technology changed everything because the amount of information flow picked up, the speed at which you could manipulate it picked up, and along the way, people became so focused on this information that they lost sight of the fact that they were buying pieces of companies. You can see this in action by looking at the

7.1: Average holding times of stocks on NYSE

average holding times of stocks on the New York Stock Exchange (NYSE).

Holding times have declined precipitously over the last 25 years. With this huge increase in the volume of information available to investors and the perceived need to act on it immediately, the time that any one stock is held has gone way down. A lot of people may be handicapped by all this technology. You could be changing your view on a company every day, every minute. In my earlier example of the financial models that took the computer an hour or more to produce, they would generally be two pages in length. Now, you get 20-page models linked to five outside sources that receive data every second and you push the button and it changes instantaneously.

I think models that are 15 to 20 pages in length are completely worthless. A one-pager that explains why you're changing some of the variables is a lot better in my view than some of this other stuff. I think technology has made things tougher in a lot of respects and the only winners are the brokers who get trading fees. Technology may also be negatively impacting the daily trading of stocks. Flash trading—super computer algorhythmic trading—now accounts for two-thirds of NYSE trades according to some estimates. So upwards of 65% of all trades are now executed between computers without taking into account the underlying companies, their fundamentals or the economy. Watch out below.

Information overload may also lead people to drop

winners too soon because they feel compelled to move on. The key is to listen to the engine that's driving your investment thesis as opposed to all the noise. A lot of people say to me, "Now look, Bob, you saw gold early. You've had it in your funds from US$250 an ounce to US$1,000 an ounce and that's great. Why don't you declare a victory and move on?" It's a question I've been asked, particularly in light of my boom thesis, many times. The reason I'm not moving on is because nothing has fundamentally changed to alter my thesis. I believe in it, so why change? In fact, the engine powering that thesis may be turning faster at this point than it has at any point in the past.

That's not to say every stock will work out. If some people have a tendency to unload their winners too early due to their desire to do something with their portfolio, there's also a tendency among investors to hang on too long. My sell criteria are simple: drop the stock if the thesis changes or if a better, stronger idea supplants it. But there will also be periods—like a baseball slugger in a hitless streak—when you've bought the wrong stock. And it's very difficult. And if you've been successful in other areas of your life either before you started investing on your own or while you're doing it, the failure is all that tougher to take.

Over the years, I have recruited and staffed three equity research teams—two in the U.S. and one in Canada—and one investment management division—Team Canada

—and most of the people I hired were A students their whole lives. Every time they've sat down to be tested, they got 95% correct or some number like that. Then they show up for this job, and good analysts, good portfolio managers bat .550 or .600 right out of the gate. That's a far cry from near-perfection. Then they hit a spell where they're batting .300 or .400. For someone who felt an 86% score on a test was a slap in the face, imagine what a 36% mark feels like?

I think failure is important because the job goes on forever. There's no clock. Most things people do are project-oriented, "We're going to get this done. We're going to work hard and work as hard as we can. We're smart. We're bright and therefore at the end we'll be done. We'll get the A and we'll move on to the next thing."

If you're a lawyer, it's getting through that case. For a carpenter, it's building that cabinet. But in stock-picking, the game never ends. Twenty-five years ago, I studied Intel as a technology analyst. My specialty was disc drives and semiconductors, if you can believe it. But what I knew then is totally irrelevant today. And someone who started looking at Intel yesterday is ahead of me, so there's no finish line.

The way to deal with your performance is to keep an even keel. You've got to look at it with a level of equanimity. You don't get too high; you don't get too low. It's a question of keeping your psychology and eliminating the emotion and the way to do that is to have a plan, to have an intelligent process that produces results and to have the discipline to stick to these things. To follow them.

Like following the plan to buy on dips: it's hard to do even for those who are fully disciplined, but knowing whether you can keep your emotions in check is key. I know a lot of guys who run pure computer portfolios and I've seen their emotion take over. One fellow I know had a terrible 2009. He runs a quant-only portfolio and the broad market was up 40% or so last year. He's down 10%.

It's scary in the worst way for him. This is a guy who's done pretty well in the past. Things were going so bad, at the start of 2010, he changed tack: he turned off the computer, a system he built for a decade and had helped him for more years than not. Now he's flying blind. That's not going to end well, I told him, but he didn't want to hear that. He said, "It's not working and I've got to do something else."

Rather than abandoning the process that's yielded success in the past or getting emotional and changing everything whole hog, I think you've got to remain even-keeled, re-examine your process and make continual improvements—slight, measured improvements. You've got to be scientific in a sense.

The toughest time for me investing was probably 1994–95. I was managing balanced money, I really got the bond portion wrong—wrong with big money. At the start of '94, bonds were in a major bear market. In

'95, the Mexican debt crisis hit and I got caught in the middle with a ton of illiquid positions. There was no getting out. The first lesson I learned was about liquidity. That was self-evident. The second thing I learned was about process and process improvements. Up until this bad stretch, I was primarily a fundamental-only investor with a solid track record. Coming out of the mess in '95, I made the decision to add quant and technical research to my investment process. I talk more about this in chapter eight, but the reason I started to draw upon the three factors lies in the fact that they're not highly correlated.

To illustrate, if three people who research a large number of stocks fundamentally, quantitatively and technically come together with a list of stocks to buy, you would look for the ones that appear on the three separate lists. When you can find an intersection among three processes that aren't highly correlated, your batting average generally goes up. What I did, in other words, was improve my investment process. I had success with the fundamental approach in the past, so instead of discarding it, I enhanced it with two new inputs.

This brings us back to the thesis of this chapter: from my experience in the mid-1990s I learned something about myself. I got a little wiser. Since I'm asking you to know yourself, I think it only fair that I turn the microscope in my direction.

What do I know about myself?

I know I invest about two-thirds the way up the risk

spectrum. I know I prefer small- and mid-cap stocks and I live for corrections, dips and underbought situations. I like to have a process, I like results that are repeatable and I like to think big picture. Big picture meaning trends, key moments and inflection points, if you will. In terms of research, I'm fundamental first but I embrace quant and tech as part of the process. And finally, I know what's right for me may not be right for you.

The key is to know thyself. And if you know managing your own investments isn't for you, hire a good manager.

CHAPTER EIGHT

Hire a good manager

"Is your manager earning his keep, or keeping your earnings?"
ANONYMOUS

My dad was many things, a war hero and a great guy among them, but he was one of the worst investors. He didn't get the chance to go to high school, he had very little money and he bought stock based only on tips from the barber. Basically, the only good stock he ever held—and I'll take some credit for it—was Exxon. I used to work for Exxon way back when and I said, "Just buy it, reinvest the dividends and don't ever pretend to trade it." It was by far the best stock he held in his life.

Needless to say, Dad would've made a terrible portfolio manager. So how do you find a good one? Or rate the one you've already got? These questions don't get sufficient attention from advisors and individual investors. They should.

Why?

Some portfolio managers are better than others. It's like any profession, but I most closely associate it with sports. Performance is easily measured in both occupations. You're going to have the good, the better and the best. The best making up, say, 10% of the total.

As you know, I'm a part-owner of the Boston Celtics. It's a dream come true. I've played basketball all my life.

In the playground, through high school and at college. I even had dreams of making it to the bigs. Or at least until I approached my college coach with a timing conflict. I had all these labs I had to take at the same time as practice and I asked him, "What do you think I should do?" He said, "Bob, I've seen your game. Go get your engineering degree."

That was it for the dream. But I'm fortunate to watch the big guys two, sometimes three times a week. And when I watch these guys, it's clear that as good as the vast majority of these players are, a handful of them fly above the rest. Think Kevin Garnett, Paul Pierce and Ray Allen. When it comes to investment management, it's no different. Some guys just live at a different altitude. At Fidelity, Peter Lynch and Bruce Johnstone of yesteryear come to mind. Today it would be Will Danoff and Joel Tillinghast. They're the cream of the crop.

Finding the best is difficult. Celtics general manager Danny Ainge fills his days with that singular pursuit: finding tomorrow's superstars. While he's comfortable with the fact that finding a real superstar happens only once in a blue moon, Ainge does feel he can identify and draft or trade for above-average performers. That's what we're trying to do here in finding you the right portfolio manager. It's less about finding the superstar and more about finding a consistent top performer.

Ainge relies on a variety of information—stats, scouts, research—to help him. One input is quantitative analysis, the use of mathematical models to predict future outcomes. Based on my experience using quant to assist in financial analysis, I was interested to see how Ainge used it to assess talent for the Celtics. The baseball guys had been doing it for years. In the 1990s, it was largely foreign to the world of basketball and the Celtics soon became a pioneer in this area. To illustrate how quant helped Ainge, let's say he was thinking of trading for, or getting as a free agent, a 34-year-old guard. Thirty four, as you know, is a little old to be running up and down the court, so Ainge's primary concern would be the productivity level of a player that age and the number of years he should offer the player in a contract. But rather than signing the player and hoping, Ainge would sit down at his computer and pull up the stats on guards who played in the NBA past the age of 34. With this as a foundation, Ainge would customize the data to the player in question. He might input factors such as the person's body mass index, the number of minutes they've played over the course of their career, how many games they've lost due to injury and so on. The mathematical model would, in turn, provide you with the odds of this player being productive in the first, second and third years of a contract. Ainge doesn't rely on this alone. A host of other factors would also be considered. But if the statistical odds of this player being productive in the third year of a proposed contract were nil, he'd want to know that.

The reason Ainge devotes time to considering this

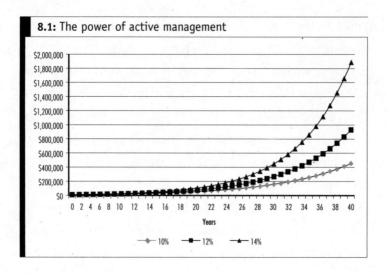

8.1: The power of active management

stuff is the same reason you should do the same when it comes to hiring a portfolio manager: it makes a difference in the outcome of the game. In basketball, it's points. In investment management, it's dollars. If each year over the life of your portfolio your portfolio manager can squeeze out one, two or even three percentage points more than the next guy, the outcome—assuming you've got a tidy sum to begin with—can be measured in tens of thousands of dollars.

So what inputs should guide you in assessing a portfolio manager?

The best way to approach this is the way institutional guys do. *Institutional* meaning companies and organizations that have large amounts of money to invest, such as pension funds. The process that institutions use to find suitable investment managers is a good template to work from to find your own manager. That's because they have a standardized method backed by stats, consultants and research to help them. Not unlike Ainge.

I got to know quite a few of the people leading this process after I spent two years as Head of Equities at Pyramis, Fidelity's institutional group, from 2004 to 2006. This was in addition to my CIO role and was based on the unfolding success of Team Canada. We had completed the hiring process, the products were largely in place and results had been good, so I was asked to run Pyramis. Over the course of the next two years, I was interviewed by a lot of people from the pension world and was exposed first-hand to the criteria they used to help them find portfolio manager talent.

Central to the selection process is a document called a Request for Proposal, or RFP. The RFP is sent to maybe half a dozen investment managers and requests key pieces of information from them. Based on the strength of the information contained in the returned RFPs, the pension consultant or company representative may book appointments with a shortlist of firms to meet them in person. The firm will probably send the CEO and/or CIO and perhaps one or two analysts.

But before consultants send out any invites, they will invest a great deal of time weighing a number of factors contained in the RFP: performance record, investment philosophy and process, research methods, resources and tracking error. I suggest do-it-yourself investors replicate the process, as should investors who use the services of a financial intermediary. The only difference is that in your case, the advisor is doing the due diligence for you: they're charging you for investment advice. The process of selecting one portfolio manager or portfolio management firm over another strikes me as being central to the manager's value proposition. Be sure to ask them what criteria they use to choose a manager for you.

Before we dig further into each of the sections of the RFP, I should mention the equity RFP template the CFA Institute Centre for Financial Market Integrity has posted on their website. The centre is the research division of the CFA Institute, the global professional organization that administers the Chartered Financial Analyst designation—the gold standard when it comes to the investment management profession. Being a template, it's rather rudimentary, but it will serve as a good starting point.

Performance record

Like a professional athlete's stats, an investment manager's performance record is the first filter you use to size up prospects. You have to know what's behind you to see what may lie ahead. I know past performance is no guarantee of future results, but if a guy has posted pretty good numbers over a long period of time and another guy has lost money more frequently than he's made money, that should carry some weight. There are a number of ways you can access this data. Check an investment company website, open a newspaper or visit Morningstar Canada and search funds for performance.

You want someone with a minimum of three to five years' experience. If one of your candidates has even more experience—say, 10 years or more—even better. You shouldn't be looking for perfection in these numbers, but rather above-average long-term performance. I've always felt a .700 batting average is a good score for fund managers. That means they'll beat their benchmark index and peer group seven times out of 10 over the life of their stewardship. The key words in the last sentence are *peer* and *benchmark*. You must look at relevant categories when you're conducting this type of examination. The funds being weighed must be in the same category (large cap, mid cap, small cap), have the same geographic investment mandate (domestic, global, international, emerging market) and be measured against the same benchmarks, or index returns. This makes for a good apples-to-apples comparison.

Once you have a good sense of how each of the managers in your pile stack up, the next step is to look at their risk-adjusted returns. Some funds are more volatile than others but wind up in the same spot. That means fund A could be up and down all year but still deliver a 10% return. Fund B, on the other hand, could be quite steady and deliberate when it comes to generating its 10% return. The choice here is between the tortoise and the hare. One fund may keep you up at night, while the other may help you sleep better. The key barometer to look at is standard deviation, which measures the degree to which a fund bounces around its benchmark index. With a good idea how bouncy or smooth the ride will be, you can choose the funds that best suit you and then discard the others. Once you've got that list, you or your advisor can take the next step: examining the investment philosophy and process.

Investment philosophy

An investment philosophy is the overall approach used to guide investment decisions. The approach could be rooted in a particular style or core beliefs of the investment management firm. One example would be a value firm where portfolio managers are only interested in buying stocks that are priced below their "intrinsic" worth, or the sum total of their assets minus liabilities. At the opposite end of the spectrum is a growth shop where managers concentrate on stocks growing faster than the economy. These managers are willing to pay a premium, or higher price per share, to participate in that growth. A third example is an investment management company that restricts its investments to companies it deems ethical, or resists commodity-based firms such as oil companies if the investment managers feel these companies have no distinct competitive advantage over one other due to their prospects being tied to a price per barrel. Knowing and understanding a firm's investment philosophy is important, because it's like a compass for your investments. If you elected to invest your money with either firm in the last example, you might have missed the boom entirely.

I believe a great investment philosophy starts with great research. Don't restrict yourself unnecessarily to any one type of stock or constrain yourself to a single style when it comes to investing. I believe almost every stock has to be considered. Peter Lynch best described this as "turning over every rock." Lynch did this through intense bottom-up fundamental research, which proved to be a hallmark of his time at Fidelity. What such research looks like for the average investor is buying only those stock that you're familiar with intimately. Stocks are companies, companies are run by people, people make strategies, people make mistakes, people need to be accountable and the stock price will reflect that. So any successful fundamental investment team must intimately know the stocks they're investing in. *Intimately* doesn't mean inside information. It means having really sharp people follow the stocks for long enough to understand the company's strategies, its people and its industry and to be able to forecast the future against expectations and against what's going on in the world. Experience counts. Seeing companies for a long time and understanding economic cycles makes a big difference.

This is what I believe. It works consistently. But

it might not be for you. That's fine. But most people aren't investing for two or three years. They're investing presumably for 10 to 30 years. And if you have ethical concerns about your investments or don't believe in investing in companies tied to commodity prices, I respect that. The point I'm making is that you should know and understand your philosophy and go from there.

Investment process

The first thing you should know about investment process—the steps taken to create a portfolio—is that it's absolutely critical because it's the most useful predictor of future outcomes. If, for instance, someone explains their process and they're finishing near last place performance-wise over 10 years, that tells you something. Alternatively, if someone explains their process and they're finishing near first place over the same time frame, it also tells you something.

The second thing you should know about process is that there is no right or wrong approach—to a degree. Each manager will, to a certain degree, have a different method to invest your money. Remember my dad and the barber? That was his investment process. I am also aware of some managers who use astrology or the lunar calendar to help them make investment decisions. That's also a process. And any process can be right for a short period of time. So if, for some reason, you bought certain stocks at a certain phase of the moon, that could be successful over a short period of time. It's probably coincidental, though it could be successful. But it won't be successful over the long term. That's the key. Institutional investors are investing for the long term. And assuming retirement is the goal for most people, that's also long term. When you're trying to determine an investment process that's right for you, be sure it stands the test of time.

My process is to research stocks in multiple ways and build portfolios based on my research. Each portfolio manager will go about this in a slightly different manner. Some will rely on fundamental research alone and apply their own personal process. That means the process is highly individualized. Peter Lynch is a perfect example at Fidelity. He was a brilliant investor, but like Kevin Garnett, he's a rare commodity. Their process is to meet with five or 10 companies a day every single day, and then take home 100 pages of research every night on another 10 companies. Every single day they keep rereading it and then they create a portfolio out of the stocks that have the best current fundamentals. There are very few people who can do that for a while. There are even fewer who can do it over an extended period. It's not so much because they become dumb or anything. It's because life catches up to them. There are kids, there are vacations. But the research waits for none of that. If you don't see your 10 companies or read about your other 10 companies, you've fallen behind and you haven't got much else to rely on.

Other managers draw on other research methods in

addition to fundamentals. Quantitative research is one. Like Ainge looking for top players, managers will use mathematical models to help them sort through the universe of stocks, identify the ones displaying the best investment potential and then overlay fundamental research to further reduce the size of the pool. They will then apply their own "buy" criteria to create a portfolio. This method is less individualized than the pure fundamentalist stock picker. There are clear steps to the process and it's easier to replicate. Still other managers may bring technical research—real-time views of the playing field—into the process. This breed of manager may weight each input differently. Some are more biased to quant, others to technical.

Personally, I like to take the process one step further. Maybe it's the engineer in me, but I'm a big believer in a multi-faceted process with standardized inputs. I think it makes it easier for the investor and the institution to repeat the results. I don't live on the same plane as Lynch. I need a standardized process. An intelligent process. It allows me to extend my investment abilities over a longer period of time and it enables me to manage more money. Using a process that is easy to repeat makes it easier to repeat the results, and that's what you want over the long term because there's no replacing a Lynch. You may think you've replaced them, but it's very unclear until after the fact.

So I'm of both worlds. I believe the investment management business works well with some of these superstars, but I'm wary of how few there are, and how difficult their job is over the long term, particularly when they get more and more money to invest. With a standardized process where you have a lot of smart individuals contributing, you're not counting on any one person for the ultimate answer. You're focusing more on the process and improving the process. So if Person 22 in the process makes a slight tweak to it for the better, it accrues to your benefit. And if you get enough of those tweaks, then this concept of process continually gets better instead of a single individual who gets worse with age.

It comes back to the notion of *kaizen*, the Japanese philosophy that says there's always a better way to do something. Mr. Johnson, Fidelity's Chairman, has a picture of the Japanese symbol for *kaizen* in his office. He's had it up there since the 1960s, long before Japanese business philosophies became popular. Everything I learned about *kaizen*, I learned from Mr. Johnson. And the notion that there are always ways to improve things— even the way you invest—stuck with me. That's why I'm so big on standardized process. Once you've put a repeatable investment method in place, you can start to improve it. Along the way, you can measure, very accurately, what works and what doesn't. By throwing out what doesn't work and focusing on what does, you can create a new, improved process and the cycle keeps repeating itself.

So have your antennae up for interpreting a manager's investment process. Think about the method—or absence of method—portfolio managers use to create portfolios. What I find is a lot of investors are sold on a bio. They're told this manager's good and this manager's bad without any consideration to the process they employ when it comes to investing.

The last thing to keep in mind is that process can change. In a lot of cases, investment management companies are bought, sold, transferred, transformed— all kinds of stuff can happen to a group of investment managers. As much as people tell you the process isn't going to change under these circumstances, it's seldom true. If the firm you currently invest with is acquired by another, be sure to update yourself on what could well be a new process.

Research

The next step in the portfolio manager search and assessment is understanding the research methods your prospective managers employ. As mentioned, I believe in multi-faceted research with the most prominent facet being fundamental. When people say they are fundamental, they mean one of two things. One way to approach fundamental research is to work top-down: you predict what the world is going to look like and then you research to find the best stocks in a particular area that will do well in that environment. So in a falling interest rate environment, you may choose to invest in more banks and utilities because both are interest-rate sensitive.

A bottom-up fundamentalist, on the other hand, will research all investable stocks and choose to invest in those deemed to have the greatest opportunity to grow.

Of the two, top-down is a far more efficient way to do things. All it takes is one guy at the top to decide where the group should focus its time and energy. So nobody covers anything else. If the call is right, it's going to end up being fairly brilliant and efficient. But I find it difficult to work exclusively from the top-down approach for two reasons. First, it negates what's going on in the real world. There may be plenty of "good" stocks you're going to overlook simply because they're not in the sector you deem to have the greatest potential. Second, if you make the wrong call, the whole portfolio is wrong. In contrast, when you take a bottom-up view, you've got everything covered. To flip the previous example, even though interest rates may be rising, you may still want to own a bank if its growth potential is good.

Bottom-up fundamental stock pickers are obligated to learn everything they can about a stock, the industry it inhabits and the competition it faces. We spend hours, days, weeks and even years assessing companies to determine where they stand in terms of sales, profits, new product launches, expansion plans, layoffs, debt, cash on hand, how they put cash to work and how they don't. And then there's current stock price, historical stock price and, most important, future stock price. What matters is what you think is going to happen to the share price and the best way to figure that out is through fundamental, bottom-up research. The tough part is that the fundamental work is hard. It's also extremely intensive in terms of manpower. But it's worth the work because the payoff is highest if you get it right.

That was the story behind Research in Motion, or RIM. We, as a team, researched it way, way back when. I mean, you could almost call us early pioneers of RIM. We looked at it when it was really nothing more than a kind of radio frequency attachment company. Before it was this fancy phone that everyone now thinks of as a BlackBerry, it was a high-tech pager. The key to it was the battery and antenna connection. It had a stronger signal and longer battery life and through fundamental research we predicted it was going to turn into something great. That was the thesis years and years ago, probably more than a decade ago. We followed RIM continuously as the thesis grew stronger until it morphed into a cell phone powerhouse.

There are actually very few companies that grow like that. We tend to remember them because they make us wealthy, but of the hundreds and, in the U.S., thousands of small companies, very few actually grow as advertised. Most get stuck. Constant monitoring and fundamental research helps you determine which companies will likely go nowhere and which may prosper.

An example of fundamental research in action is the Fidelity Canadian Disciplined Equity Fund. The fund, which was one of the first products I launched and managed after becoming CIO, was created in September 1998. It was one of the industry's first sector-neutral funds, meaning it had exposure to all 10 sectors of the S&P/TSX. By doing so, it alleviated the need for the investor to make a call on which sectors of the index displayed the greatest promise. I found it interesting that some advisors dismissed it at the time as an index fund because of its exposure to the entire benchmark. But within each sector, there are always opportunities to find mispriced companies through fundamental research. So, working with the analysts, we put a portfolio together that had stocks from every sector at all times.

For example, when gold was at US$250 an ounce we had a lot of gold stocks. Few other managers could say the same thing in 1999. As you will recall from chapter two, the gold sector was out of favour in 1999—it was in the trash can—but from a fundamental perspective, there were a lot of opportunities here and the fund's all-sector mandate obligated us to find the best. It was a similar story in the technology sector. Even when it hit a high point in 2000, we had exposure, but it was limited to the least risky in the sector. So pure research: that's the key. You know, you can own really aggressive technology stocks or not so aggressive, really conservative ones. Back in the day when technology was burning brightest, we would own less aggressive stocks than Nortel.

The month after I left the fund, it received the 2009 Canada Lipper Fund Award as the top-performing

fund of the decade in the Lipper Category of Canadian
Equity. The results speak to the power of fundamental
research. The success of the fund over 12 years didn't
come down to any one story or any one idea. It was about
this intimate knowledge of the companies we invested in.
But fundamental isn't the only research method I employ.
There's also quantitative and technical.

Quantitative research, as mentioned in the Danny
Ainge story, is all about numbers, mathematical models
and relationships between things. The analyst, or "quant"
as they're called, generally comes from the world of math,
physics or engineering. They have PhDs and are good
computer programmers. As investors, their view of the
world comes from looking at it in reverse. They drive
the car by looking in the rear-view mirror. They look for
patterns in historical numbers and based on what they
see in these numbers, they will determine whether a
company will outperform over the coming months and
years. Quantitative research allows you to use computers
to look at lots of different valuation metrics, sort them
out for each individual industry or company and see
which ones have worked in the past and flag you when
they're signalling buy. The head of quant I brought into
Team Canada was this guy Peter Millington. After
meeting Millington and seeing his work, team members
would comment, "What is this guy, a rocket scientist?"
And when I hired him, he actually was a rocket scientist.
He got his PhD from the Massachusetts Institute of

Technology in jet propulsion and he left Lockheed Martin to join us.

The marriage between quantitative and fundamental analysis is best exemplified by the Fidelity Systematic Equity Fund, which Millington started. A pension product available to institutional investors only, the fund is one of the highest-ranked institutional portfolios in Canada.

The third type of research I use in my process is technical. Technical researchers aren't interested in company fundamentals or historic quantitative analysis. Their sole focus is the market or a stock and how it's performing now and in its past. They discern movements in a stock's price, the volumes (or amount of selling), moving averages, top and bottom prices and so on. So a technical analyst may flag a company as an investment candidate not necessarily knowing what the company does or any of the financials attached to it.

All three analysts are striving for the same result—to identify stocks that will rise or fall—but all three employ different methods to reach a conclusion. Although I'm a fundamentalist at heart, I believe the best stock picks become clear when you leverage each research platform: quantitative, technical and fundamental. The three methods complement each other and that's the core of the research process I believe in. My belief stems from the fact that your investment mosaic will be incomplete without considering all three.

When I was discussing key moments in the previous

chapter and cited the example of buying back into the market in 2009 following the financial crisis, it was technical research and the signals it was sending that helped motivate my action. As you will recall, the market had fallen precipitously and corporate futures across virtually all industries were gloomy. If you were a pure fundamentalist, I'm not so sure you would have bought the market at that time. Things just looked too bad for companies going forward. Conversely, if you were a pure quantitative investor, you would have bought into the market earlier than spring 2009 when the markets were off 20%. But again, as you know, the markets continued to fall another 30% to 40%. So if you had relied on quant signals alone, you would have been early. Technically, however, it signalled a big buy, a big bottom in the spring of 2009 and sometimes part of the game is trusting one, two or three of your research approaches. Sometimes the fundamental starts the process, other times it's the quantitative and still other times, the technical. Regardless of which method kicks off the process, I ensure the other methods are subsequently engaged.

So if ABC company has been flagged by one of the quantitative models because it has reached a valuation metric that suggests it's a buy, I would want to ensure I take a look at the fundamental research being done on the company. You then have the industry analyst call or visit the company because they are the expert in whatever industry ABC is in. The industry analyst has the context, they know what competitors are doing and they generally have a good handle on the trends impacting the business. The analyst would speak with the company, create an independent financial model to try to predict the future, or at least enough of it to fill out next year's income statement and balance sheet for that company. And that's really what you're trying to do. As you fill out your estimate of next year's income statement, let's say you find growth. Growth in excess of what is the consensus view or word on the street.

The next step for the professional equity analyst is to codify their views by creating research notes. A research note gives the managers an idea of what's new with the firm and how it relates to the current investment thesis, or rationale for why you should or shouldn't continue to invest in the company under review. The key section in the note is entitled "Investment Thesis." It's no more than a couple of bullet points identifying the most salient pieces of information from the tons of data you've acquired. What do you know that's different? What's your angle? What are your key investment points? They will change for each company under consideration. For example, the bullet points on RIM coming up with a brand new, really cool product are definitely going to be different than the bullet points on Canadian Pacific, where you're not going to find any new products or marketing push.

The thesis will also change depending upon the development stage of the company. To use RIM for example, let's say the investment thesis is "Buy RIM because the new Storm is going to exceed expectations. It's a game changer and their gross margin on it is higher than their other products." Then the story two weeks or two months later could be very simple. It could be just one bullet point, "Storm continues to exceed expectations."

So you've laid the groundwork and now the follow-up is on track. Analysts will update a note at least three or four times a year. That's a minimum. For larger companies like a RIM, you might get a refreshed note every month because an analyst is likely meeting someone from the company every month and there's a lot of news flow and very frequent updates.

With the fundamental and quantitative research up to date and complete, the final and third pillar in my investment process would be technical. Technicians are also following the stock, and their conclusions are compared and contrasted with the fundamental and quantitative research. Technicians are predicting your price movements from factors such as trading volumes, sentiment, and perhaps even the visual pattern of stock prices. The next step consists of the three analysts presenting their findings at an investment team meeting. In some instances, the quant and tech guys would present after the fundamental guys. It can get pretty feisty when one researcher says "sell" just after another poured their heart out for a buy. Particularly if the fundamentalist disagreed with the other two. That happens. But there are also instances when the fundamentalist and one of the other two agree. On rare occasions, all three will agree. To me that was the Holy Grail because each view—fundamental, quant, technical—is uncorrelated with the others. In other words, the fundamentalist may say "Yes" to a stock. One "Yes" out of three may be sufficient rationale for a stock investment. Two out of three certainly is. And three out of three— multiple hits—tells me there's a chance of a home run. That's what happened to gold in 1999.

Using multiple research platforms—fundamental, quant and technical—is the approach I took when I created the Pyramis Concentrated Market Neutral Fund for Fidelity. It's an American domiciled fund and, as with the Systematic Equity Fund, available to pension plans only. The Pyramis fund, which engages in both long and short strategies, was one of Pyramis's most successful funds and epitomized my investment process. More than simply a gaudy performance, Pyramis's success shows that learning about yourself, assembling the correct resources and acting on your philosophy is a way to create value in almost any market environment.

As you can see, there's a wide variety of research methods an investment manager can employ. Some focus on fundamental. Others a mix of quant and fundamental. At Fidelity, it was up to the manager and sometimes the fund's mandate how much weight—if any—would be given to the various methods. My objective was to simply make all the research available. I think that if the organization hires and retains great people this suite of research will provide a long-term advantage in the marketplace. Worldwide, for example, Fidelity covers more than 90% of companies on global indexes, conducting over 8,000 in-house company meetings and annually producing over 30,000 research reports. This is a tremendous amount of research. Further, it's shared across the globe. As a portfolio manager, if I wanted to know the latest thinking on European oil companies, I could easily, I mean literally in seconds, pull up all of the ratings, research notes and the most recent industry review from Fidelity internal sources. Without even having to call someone, I could do that. It was the same with investment-grade bonds, high-yield bonds, Asian stocks, whatever. That is truly an admirable global process.

Sometimes you may get a note from across the ocean that may seem irrelevant to you, but it may be important news for others in the organization. That's key, too. I remember a note from a researcher in Asia covering a company that supplied equipment to a prominent Canadian technology company. Now, if you weren't invested in the company or weren't considering an investment, the note would pass without mention. But in Canada the note was well read because it concerned a Canadian company. The researcher commented that the Asian-based firm's sales to the Canadian company were dropping. If the Canadian company was purchasing less, were they, in turn, selling less? Coincidentally, the company had a scheduled meeting with us in Boston. I recall the meeting vividly because there was no mention of declining sales. If anything, the mood was upbeat and everything was running full out. We didn't make mention of the note or of the information we had from Asia. Rather, we kept quiet but began to take a closer, fundamental look, and over the course of the next several weeks, we started to unwind some of our positions. Not all, mind you, but a good many. Ultimately, this technology company declared bankruptcy. We benefited from thinking globally and paying attention.

Resources

Resources—the human resources, technology and systems available to a firm—compose the third area of interest for institutional investors. But before you pull out your yard stick and conclude bigger is better, it's important to be comparing apples to apples, similar to how we compared the performance records of investment managers. A small investment manager, such as a hedge fund that's narrowly focused in a particular area, can be well resourced with two to five people. They may, for instance, be looking to manage a relatively small amount of money—a billion dollars or less—and in a narrowly defined category such as small-cap or a less-than-global region such as Canada. They don't need 40 guys to do that. In fact, that would be counterproductive.

You want to compare apples to apples. Fidelity's

premise since it was started over 60 years ago has always been to offer and cover everything and do it on a big scale. That means they have funds in every category, cover every investable stock and are prepared to handle enormously large sums of money. Today, Fidelity manages over US$1.3 trillion as at June 30, 2009, has over 400 stand-alone mutual funds and over 20 million investors worldwide. Those are big numbers. It's only fair to compare Fidelity to other firms that are managing a lot of money in a global context or who are hoping to manage a lot of money, and then ask, "Do you have enough resources to do everything?" The response the investor should be looking for is, "Yes, before we offer anything, we will have the resources in place." Build the team and ensure the necessary resources are in place before any products are offered.

No matter the size of the firm, though, you can ask that same question—"Do you have enough resources to do everything?"—to determine if a firm can meet your needs. You could ask that same question of smaller organizations that, instead of specializing, have a lineup purporting to do everything. Then the real question is, "Do you *really* have the resources to do everything? Or are you giving me an international fund where the manager is in Toronto and has no proprietary research in London, Hong Kong or Tokyo?" That's a fair question.

And if a firm wants to manage tens of billions of dollars and claims to be a primarily fundamental research shop, then the next question an investor and advisor should ask is "Do you have the manpower to fulfill a fundamental equity research commitment?"

The key question to ask is whether the investment management organization's product offering, asset size and philosophy confirm the resource level. Keep in mind that experience counts. Managers and analysts with experience and demonstrated success may, in fact, have many times more worth than poorly trained, inexperienced analysts. Moreover, if the product offering is limited and the research process includes multiple sources (fundamental, quantitative and technical), then the amount of resources required from any one discipline will likely be less than if all sources were unavailable.

Tracking error

Tracking error is another important evaluation tool when hiring a manager or sizing up the one you've already got. Tracking error measures the difference between a manager's portfolio and benchmark returns. This does not appear on the CFA Institute's RFP, but I think it's important because you're paying someone to invest for you and if they are simply "buying" the same stocks that reside in an index, you're simply not getting value for money.

Tracking error is said to be high or low. If you measure the tracking error of an index fund whose job is to mirror the returns of a benchmark, you would want extremely low tracking error. The opposite is true when it comes to active management where the manager is paid to outperform the index. In this case, you would want high tracking error. If, however, you see low tracking error in an actively managed fund, it could be cause for concern, as the fees you are paying may not be justified. In this situation, managers are often labelled "closet indexers."

The factors that affect tracking error can range from the number of stocks in a portfolio to the size of the investment universe and the amount of assets in a fund. I'll touch on each of these factors and identify ways to obtain tracking error measures.

Although there is some disagreement among financial academics as to whether there's a correlation between the number of stocks in a portfolio and tracking error, in my experience, fewer stocks lead to higher tracking error. If, for instance, there are 500 stocks on a benchmark index and the manager owns 250 of them, I have seen greater tendencies to deliver returns more similar to the index. What is the optimal amount? I'm not sure, but I've always been biased to more concentrated portfolios where I think there is greater likelihood for outperformance. Look for portfolios that have between 50 and 100 stocks.

The size of the investment universe in terms of market capitalization is also important. Market capitalization is determined by adding up the value—market cap—of each company on an index. Small-cap market indexes will, as a result, have a much smaller market cap than a large-cap index. Small-cap active managers will generally display higher tracking error than those who invest in large-cap markets. This isn't always the case, but it's something you should be aware of when looking for tracking error.

Another determinant of tracking error is the size of the fund itself. The larger funds become, the more likely they are to look like the market. That's because funds can't hold more than 10% of a company without publicly announcing it, so the manager is almost forced to buy bigger and bigger companies to remain below the threshold. That tends to lead to big index names and low tracking error. Again, it's difficult to say how big is too big, but take a look at the portfolio's top ten holdings and the percentages ascribed to each. If it reads the same as the index, you may be better off investing in a low-cost index fund.

The ideal is to find a small fund pursuing a small niche in the market. This is where I've seen the potential for outsize gains. If you have an adviser, be sure to ask about the tracking error associated with fund recommendations. And if you invest yourself, there are financial websites that will give you that information. It's quick, it's easy and you may enjoy substantial savings or gains over the course of your investing life by checking.

Finally, the manner in which a portfolio manager is compensated is worthy of consideration. Advisors can get a handle on this by asking the investment management firm they're dealing with while individual investors can simply write an email or letter requesting an answer. Regardless of the answer, I want to stress that this is not a deal breaker, but it should be viewed as an additional input into your overall decision-making. Simply put, there are some firms that create a compensation scheme that's more aligned to investors while other firms create schemes more aligned to the firm. Let me give you an example of what's shareholder-friendly and what's not.

A lot of firms calculate their portfolio managers' pay as a percentage of assets. Assets could be the total amount of money under management at the firm or the amount of money in a particular fund. In some instances, managers and analysts receive compensation from both pools—fund and firm assets. In such a case, a manager would be rewarded for asset gathering. Now, you could argue that the way to attract assets is through good performance, and that's true. But there are plenty of other ways to raise asset levels that have nothing to do with performance. Marketing can, for instance, play a big role. If a firm supports a particular product with a large marketing budget to create sales brochures, stage promotional events and support a portfolio manager road show, the firm is positioning the fund to grow assets independent of performance. Advertising—print or television—will, when effective, provide a similar lift. Sales departments are also good at their jobs. Quarterly or semi-annually, heads of sales will meet to determine what funds they want to highlight and showcase to advisors. In each of these examples, assets can grow even if performance is bad or middling, and portfolio managers will be paid regardless. I don't think that's right. I've always thought portfolio managers and analysts should be paid based on how they did for investors.

The hedge fund compensation model is a good place to start when thinking about models that work for investors. It's not perfect, but in essence the portfolio managers and analysts are not going to get paid unless you, the investor, do well. Hedge funds typically follow the "two and 20" rule. The investment team will earn 2% compensation on assets and take 20% of your excess return. So if your fund earns $1 in excess return, the management team will take 20 cents. There is strong incentive, in other words, to do well for investors. As I said, it's not perfect but it's a step in the right direction.

The best situation, I think, is when the portfolio manager is rewarded only if the investor is rewarded. It's something you should become familiar with when judging investment managers.

We've covered a lot in the preceding pages: performance record, investment philosophy and process, research, resources and tracking error. To sum up, what do you look for in a good portfolio manager? What's the ideal? The ideal is one that has a believable, well-resourced, established investment process and philosophy that makes sense to you. The portfolio manager and analysts should be on your side, meaning their compensation is based on you doing well. Their results should be consistently good and tracking error should be high enough to put some distance between the fund and its index. That's the ideal.

> ### For hire
>
> Hiring a good manager can be as simple as asking your advisor or the fund company the right questions and understanding the answers. You might not like the answers. All the better. Move on to the next guy.
>
> 1. Can you provide me with the fund's performance record versus its peers?
> 2. How would you describe the manager's investment philosophy in your own words?
> 3. What process does the manager use to identify stocks to buy/ sell?
> 4. What resources (analysts, portfolio managers) support the fund?
> 5. What is the manager's tracking error and are they bonused on assets, performance or both?

That's why there are some huge institutional companies in the U.S. such as Wellington and Cap Guardian that continue to attract money because of their process and good long-term performance.

Finally, some advisors and investors may feel uncomfortable broaching these subjects with their investment managers or are unsure what to ask. Let me tackle the first aspect: discomfort. I can tell you from first-hand experience that I welcomed any and all questions relating to these subjects, whether they were put to me by a pension consultant in a boardroom or by investors after a luncheon. I think the only CIOs who would be reluctant to deal with these questions are the ones who don't have the answers. That, in itself, speaks volumes.

Admittedly, it's a little tougher for individual investors to ask questions of a firm when they don't have the same privileges as advisors. I encourage you to write. A simple email or letter will get the job done. Address it to the CIO if you like, or client services. I promise you it will get answered. Again, if it doesn't, that speaks volumes.

CHAPTER NINE

How will you know the boom is over?

All good things must come to an end.
ENGLISH PROVERB

I could see the Bank of New England (BNE) building from my Fidelity office window in downtown Boston. I would look out at the building's 40-plus storeys and the bank's blue-and-white beacon logo burning bright kept me company many a night when I stayed late at the office. In 1991, the bank failed due to aggressive mortgage lending and was liquidated. The failure made headlines because BNE's failure was the largest since the 1989 collapse of Mcorp, based in Dallas and the 1988 collapse of the First Republicbank Corporation, also of Dallas. BNE was not the only bank in the region with problems, leading to fears that large depositors might quickly withdraw money from other banks in Boston, including the Bank of Boston, the Shamut Bank and Fleet/Norstar Financial Group.[1]

It wasn't a good time to be invested in banks, or any sectors for that matter. The bears were prowling and the mood at the portfolio managers' meeting was anything but upbeat. At the time, Bruce Johnstone, an icon of value investing, ruled the roost, and if you totalled the number of portfolio managers in the meeting and the funds they managed, it represented about half of Fidelity assets. Jeff Vinik was running Fidelity Contra Fund and was seated beside me. Vinik, an incredible money manager who went on to manage Fidelity Magellan Fund from 1992 to 1996 producing a cumulative 83% return, is a cut above most— including myself. He may be best known to Canadians as the owner of the Tampa Bay Lightning hockey team. The majority of the discussion at the meeting was devoted to the BNE failure, the resulting financial panic and the difficult investment environment.

But before the meeting had started, Vinik stood up and said the seeds of the next boom will be sown in this bust. The room went silent. He continued by saying he was considering a big stake in Magna International to prove his point. He bought the stock around US$1.50 and within three years it was up thirtyfold to US$45. He was the only one at the table with the conviction to buy at the time.

I still remember his words: a bust helps sow the seeds for the boom. And I think his sentiment can be flipped to describe what will happen to the current boom. It will sow the seeds of the bust.

When that will occur, I don't know exactly. But I know the boom has plenty of room to run for the better part of 10 years. I figure it's a three-act play. The first act was the period from 2001 to 2007. Then we had an intermission. We come back in 2010 and we're in the second act.

We're setting the stage for the third act. And you know what? We may have another intermission before it's all over. Hopefully it won't be another fire-in-the-theatre intermission like we had in 2008, but we may have another. I think that's okay.

The key is to catch the second act and part of the third, and you're well timed for that. So how will you know it's over? I guess the fat lady will sing. The notes she hits will be the signs. Just as there were signs indicating the start of the boom, there will be signs heralding its end. The tough part is hearing them and then acting upon them by

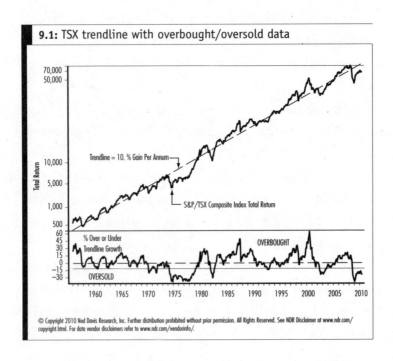

9.1: TSX trendline with overbought/oversold data

picking up your program and heading for the parking lot to drive home.

So what will the signs be?

To answer that question, I think we have to break the discussion in two. The first part of our analysis will focus on the broader market. In other words, what signs will suggest the S&P/TSX is ready for a fall? Once we have a better understanding of what to look for in the benchmark index, we can turn our attention to specific sectors. Each will send different signals. It will be important to be on the lookout for these signals as they relate to gold, oil and agriculture.

To begin, let's go back to the trendline chart I've referred to more than once. Just as it tells us when the market is oversold, it also tells us when it is overbought. When the market starts to enter the 35%–40% over-bought area, it will be a major bell-ringing signal that we are getting close to the end. This was the case in 1956, 1987 and 2000. If we reach 25,000 on the S&P/TSX, bells should be going off in your head. Keep in mind, there's no law of nature that says you can't be 45% or 50% overbought and so on. But when you get to that level, as we've talked about many times, you're starting to be the sucker in a sucker's bet.

Another overarching signal that things are topping out will be valuation metrics. Yes, the traditional ones will be stretched—that's part and parcel of any boom—but that doesn't concern me. What does make me anxious is the creation of *new* valuation metrics. Think back to the Internet bubble. The forces inflating the bubble were many but the key was the novelty and "life-changing possibilities" behind the birth and growth of the Internet. Caught up by the excitement and fascination with the new technology at the time, many companies shot up in value literally overnight by simply having an "e-" prefix on their name and a "dot-com" at the end. Some of the more memorable flame-outs were eToys, pets.com and Boo.com. One of the arguments made at the time for investing in dot-coms was that traditional valuations such as price-to-earnings and price-to-sales ratios no longer mattered. What mattered was the number of eyeballs a particular company or website could attract. One of the popular ones, as I recall, was the introduction of a price-to-population metric. In the case of the coming boom, when you start hearing financial commentators and pundits creating new metrics to support current share prices across gold, oil, agriculture and the market as a whole, that will be a signal that the boom is coming to an end.

Another marker will be an intense rush of investment capital into gold, oil and agriculture. Just as venture capitalists started writing what were essentially blank cheques to fund a wide range of Internet start-up companies, you'll see the chequebook come out again to support new gold, oil and agriculture companies and ventures. That means a jump in initial public offerings (IPOs) of new exploration companies, oil drillers and all kinds of things like that, whereas in the Internet boom it was tech, telecoms and dot-coms. These IPOs will be off the beaten track of historic development, so lands will be staked in hitherto undeveloped areas. You'll see these stocks oversubscribed and in early days of trading they may jump 25%, 50% or more. You may see similar occurrences in China, Russia and other leading developing countries where their stock markets reach crazy valuations and IPOs become the order of the day.

The flow of money into Canadian equity mutual funds will also pick up speed as the fat lady sings. Earlier I lamented how Canadians allocated the majority of their investments in the U.S. and Europe starting in 2005. I think you'll see that reverse itself during the boom. Two to three years later, the taps will completely open, flooding domestic funds of all kinds but primarily those that are 100% equity-focused. Whenever one category heats up, it attracts money. The closer it gets to a boil, ever-increasing amounts are added. There were intense spikes in fund flows with the biggest peaks in 1999 and 2000 as investors piled in. For those people, it was not a happy ending. As I've said, you've got to zig when others zag. When we get a couple of years of significant Canadian equity mutual fund purchases followed by ever-stronger flows, it will be a signal we are nearer the end than the beginning. A similar pattern should evidence itself in country-specific funds invested in Brazil, Russia, India and China. The same goes for broader BRIC and emerging market funds just as when the hot money moved into Internet, telecommunications and technology sector funds at the turn of the century.

Finally, you should heighten your awareness to what's happening around you. Broadly speaking, the top of any market is marked with a wave of enthusiasm that pervades our everyday life. When you hear about or know people who are quitting their jobs to trade oil stocks, buy and sell gold futures, or corn, wheat and so on, that's usually indicative of a top. As was the case with the Internet boom, you will hear people talking about the price of oil, the price of gold and how well they've profited from these areas. In the financial press, you'll read how strong things are, how good things are and how great Canada is. This will crossover into the general press, making front page news. You'll hear the chatter at parties, similar to what you heard during the housing boom in the U.S. or the tech and telecom boom before it. People will be talking about the stocks they own and the funds they own. I remember cocktail parties where people were boasting about the housing boom in the U.S. and how this house sold for X or mine's worth three times X. It will be eerily familiar to the stories at the peak in 2000 about plumbers who were day trading dot-com stocks.

It takes a while for the froth to build. It's not in just one marker, it's not in just one month, and it builds upon itself. The housing bubble built for years in the U.S., as did the rise in the markets in 1981. Importantly, when enough of these markers evidence themselves and it comes time to take money off the table, you won't get the exact day, week or month right—no one ever does. But it shouldn't matter much if you got in at the early-to-mid stages because you'll have made a lot of money, taken it off the table and left other people at the tippy top. For those who stepped off the tech-telecom thing in mid-to-late 1999 and missed March 2000 and the ensuing months, they would be happy, right? They might have had a couple of months where they felt like dummies, but you just have to trust that if you are a long-term investor, getting out is the correct move to make.

One last thought before we move into the sector-specific markers that will herald the end of the boom in gold, oil and agriculture. I think you'll find that as these commodities drive up in price, companies will start to increase supply. Demand may look insatiable at first glance, but if you look deeper, you'll notice supply ticking upward. So you'll see oil at US$100 again or whatever the number will be, but you'll start to hear about more oil wells coming on stream. You'll hear about gold being found somewhere, maybe on the moon or something. At the right price, supply always rises to meet demand. And then the boom is over.

The Internet frenzy is, yet again, instructive. One major cause that led to the bursting of the bubble was oversupply. The Intels, Ciscos, Nortels and other mid-and-small-cap chip, equipment and fibre optic manufacturers were running flat out to supply product to the raft of tech, Internet and telecommunications companies. The Y2K switchover further accelerated the spending on—and supply of—equipment. When December 31, 1999, passed without incident, businesses of all stripes and manner had the equipment they needed. In fact, you're just starting to see companies renew business spending 10 years later in 2010. It will be a similar story in commodities. Stocks and markets will be bid up, the bubble will inflate and then supply will come on stream in a big way. So that kills it.

Gold

There will be a number of big tipoffs when gold is reaching its top. The first will be a halt in gold purchases by the BRICs and other developing countries. Over the past 10 years, they have been big gold buyers. Their motivation lay in a desire to sufficiently diversify their foreign exchange reserves with an asset other than paper currencies such as the euro, yen and U.S. dollar.

Of greatest concern is the value of the slumping U.S. dollar. From early March through late November 2009, the dollar slid almost 17% against a basket of major currencies—the biggest decline for the dollar in any eight-month period since 1986.[2] The reasons are many and have been well documented, but the huge amount of

U.S. dollars being printed and the projected size of U.S. federal deficits has left developing countries with the view that gold is a much surer investment than the greenback. The metal is, in other words, resuming its traditional role as a store of value. This is illustrated by the U.S. dollar's share of global currency reserves, which fell in the fourth quarter of 2009 to a decade low of 62.8%. (In the second quarter of 2001, the dollar share was 73%.)[3] I think developing countries will continue to buy gold until their gold assets as a percentage of foreign currency reserves equate that of the average developed country.

In 2010, the international average of gold as a percentage of foreign currency reserves was 10.2%.[4] Many developed countries, particularly those in the European Union, exceed that amount by a wide margin. As of September 2010, France has 65.7% of its foreign reserves in gold; Germany, 67.4%; Italy, 66.2%; the Netherlands, 55.8%; and Spain, 35.9%.[5] Although I don't expect to see developing countries reach these levels, they've been playing catch-up through the 2000s and the buying was accelerating at the close of the decade.

From 2000 to 2010, China has increased the amount of gold it holds in reserve from 395 tonnes to 1,054. This made the country the world's sixth largest holder of gold bullion.[6] But with an estimated US$1.95 trillion in foreign currency reserves, gold represented just 1.9% of China's overall reserves. The Chinese government has publicly stated it would like to boost its gold reserves to

6,000 tons within three to five years and 10,000 tons in eight to 10 years.[7]

On November 3, 2009, India bought 200 tons from the IMF at a cost of US$6.7 billion. The purchase moved India up to the ninth largest government gold owner but still a long way from the 10% held by developed countries. Of India's total US$268.3 billion in foreign currency assets, gold represented US$13.3 billion, including the most recent purchase.[8] That works out to about 4% of total foreign reserves. I expect India will double its gold assets during the coming boom. When that happens, India's central bank will put away its chequebook.

Also in the fall of 2009, Russia's central bank added 15.5 tonnes of gold to its reserves. Mexico, Venezuela and the Philippines are also buying gold, albeit in smaller amounts.[9] The stated reasons in each case were to diversify holdings and manage risk to the U.S. dollar. When these and other developing countries have reached the 10% plateau, the foot will come off the gold-buying pedal, which is a sure sign the boom in gold is coming to an end. Looking forward, the Swiss bank UBS surveyed 80 central bank reserve managers in 2010 and found nearly a quarter believed gold would become the most important reserve asset in the next 25 years.[10]

Another important recent demand driver fuelling the boom in gold has been inflation, or rather the fear of inflation. Gold is well-known for retaining its value in terms of the real goods it can buy. In 1900, for instance, gold sold for an average of US$20.67 an ounce. Adjusted for inflation, that works out to be about US$500 an ounce. From 2003 to 2008, the price of gold averaged around US$600. So the real price of gold has endured for more than 100 years. That sharply contrasts with the real value of most currencies, including the British pound, Japanese yen and U.S. dollar, which have significantly declined over time.

Since the financial crisis began, economic stress, ballooning budget deficits and unprecedented stimulus plans have led investors to conclude that inflationary times may be around the corner. This has led to significant gold buying—bullion and otherwise—which has created a strong tailwind behind the price of gold. Subsiding inflation fears among investors—real or perceived—will prove to be another sign that gold's trajectory is changing.

That's the demand side of the equation. In terms of supply, gold could turn to bust if global gold production increases significantly. That's a big *if*. Gold production has been in decline since 2000–2001 and now stands at the same place it did in 1996. South African production alone has been halved since peaking in 1970. This despite record gold prices and Herculean efforts to find it, but that's the key point: over the past 150 years—since the California gold rush of 1848—gold production has risen, in some cases dramatically, following a rise in the price of gold. Higher prices lead to greater capital investment and exploration. As mentioned, exploration spending dropped significantly during the 1990s as the price of gold languished. That has reversed itself with exploration budgets tripling from 2000 to 2010.[11] Potential gold deposits have been identified on the Pacific Ring of Fire, in sub-Saharan Africa, the greenstone belt of South America, and Kazakhstan and Uzbekistan. In many instances, however, these are low-grade deposits. In fact, ore grades have fallen from around 12 grams per tonne in 1950 to nearer three grams in the U.S., Canada and Australia.[12] Further, it takes, on average, about 10 years to move from discovery to extraction. Nevertheless, the supply side of the equation is one that warrants mention particularly when we're looking at a potentially decade-long boom.

Another sign I'll be looking for to tell me gold is losing its lustre lies outside the demand-supply equation. Remember the "once in a blue moon" chart that tracked the price of gold against the performance of the Dow? If the headlines are swirling about the price of gold, it may be instructive to compare price against points. If you see a Dow-to-gold ratio of 2 to 1 or maybe even 1 to 1, it's probably time to be reaching for your program. So you've got a great 100-year-old marker to help you decide when gold's boom is over.

The price of gold adjusted for inflation is another historically good barometer in predicting gold's fall. Even though gold has broken through the US$1,300 an ounce threshold it would still have to rise to US$2,287 an

9.2: Dow vs. gold

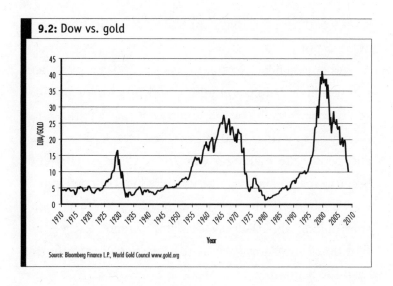

Source: Bloomberg Finance L.P., World Gold Council www.gold.org

ounce in today's dollars to match its previous record high set in 1980.[13] When we see the price of gold adjusted for inflation enter that neck of the woods, I think the odds of it falling will be greater than of it rising. So gold would have to reach the general vicinity of US$2,000 to US$2,300 an ounce in today's dollars to reach this point.

The final marker on gold harks back to something I touched on earlier in our discussion of broad metrics. When you start to see new valuation metrics for gold, I think the punch bowl will be getting pretty close to empty. I compared it to the dot-com bubble when people moved from traditional price-to-earnings and price-to-sales ratios to assess companies and embraced things like price-to-population to justify high share prices. I remember hearing some analysts say, "Wow, this company is only $20 per pop. That's cheap, because this other one is $80 per pop."

When you take two crazy numbers and compare them, you can justify almost anything. With gold, for instance, you may start seeing people compare its price to the global money supply. So if gold has reached US$3,000 an ounce and people are making a case for it to go to US$6,000 because it's still just a fraction of global money supply, you've changed the metric completely. When people stop talking about supply, demand, foreign reserves and traditional measures such as that, we're closer to the end than the beginning.

Oil

Alberta's oil sands are a wonder. I've been there a couple of times as both an oil analyst and a portfolio manager. Most recently, I had the chance to visit Fort McMurray in 2000. Aside from the cold temperatures, the thing I remember the most are the trucks and the size of their tires. It's a sight you never forget. Nor is the sight of the sands and the potential that lies there. In total, the oil sands reserves are estimated at 171.8 billion barrels or about 13% of total global oil reserves. That places Canada second behind Saudi Arabia in world ranking of proven oil reserves by country.[14] The key to being in the league of the Saudis was realizing the tar sands' potential, something that had proven elusive ever since exploratory leases were first issued in the late 1950s. Since then, the number of companies that are actively producing or planning production has changed many times due to the high costs associated with extraction and processing.

Conventional oil is described as being light or heavy. The light stuff flows naturally from the ground to the surface or is brought up using pump jacks. Heavy oil is thicker. It needs help to come out of the ground and pump jacks usually do the trick. Oil sands, on the other hand, are a mixture of sand, water, clay and bitumen. Bitumen is oil that's too heavy or thick to flow or be raised by a pump jack. At colder temperatures—the norm for northern Alberta—the bitumen is as hard as a hockey puck. Bitumen close to the surface is mined like coal with electric shovels five storeys high extracting great amounts, which are then loaded onto the oversized dump trucks with the tires 20 feet in diameter. From there, the bitumen is crushed and the sand and clay removed with hot water. The next step is a trip to the on-site upgrader plant, which converts the bitumen into synthetic crude, which is then sent via pipeline to refineries in Edmonton and the United States.

Underground bitumen, which accounts for 80% of oil sands reserves, is removed using specialized extraction techniques. The most common system uses one well to pump steam underground to heat up and liquefy the bitumen, which is then brought to the surface using a second well. As is the case with mined bitumen, the underground stuff must be treated on-site with the upgrader before it can be hauled away to a refinery for processing.[15]

Not surprisingly, oil sands extraction is significantly more expensive and time-consuming than light or heavy oil recovery. According to the Canadian Energy Research Institute, the industry has spent about $139 billion on oil sands development between 1997 and 2010, including $20 billion in 2008 alone. Compared to the Middle East where the oil comes out of the ground like soda through a straw, these are astronomical costs. Costs that make sense only when the price per barrel is north of US$40.[16]

Current oil sands production is about 1.8 million barrels per day (bpd). The oil sands are pegged to double that by 2020.[17] When Alberta's oil sands production forecasts are realized, it will be a signal that the boom is coming to end for oil.

You can draw the same conclusion if you see shale oil extraction being undertaken once again as a means to produce crude. When I was working as a chemical engineer for Exxon in 1981–1982 at its Synthetic Fuel Division in New Jersey, we were working on a couple of big projects. This was at the tail end of the last oil boom when headlines were predicting the price of oil would go to the moon: adjusted for inflation, the prices people were talking were upward of US$200 a barrel in today's dollars, a price that gets everyone thinking about alternate sources of oil. The focus of my work was a place called Parachute, Colorado. I don't think you can find Parachute on a map, but it's about 150 miles west of Denver, deep in the Rocky Mountains. I visited it many times in the early '80s to help Exxon with their strategy to get oil from shale rock. Shale is slate-coloured rock and the oil can be seen as striated lines, or veins, through the rock. The goal was to get the oil into a form that could go to a refinery.

A common headache for integrated oil companies like Exxon is to get the crude into a form that they could send directly to a refinery. Oil companies make their margins on finished products: gasoline, motor oil, kerosene and diesel, for example. Light sweet crude is the easy stuff. You take it out of the ground and send it right to the refinery. Shale oil—like oil sands bitumen—requires an extra step. It has to be "refined" before it's refined. So at Parachute, you not only have to crush mountains to extract small amounts of oil, but you also have to build a refinery on site before the stuff gets processed the traditional way. This was going to be a good-to-go engineering marvel. Very similar to the oil sands. In addition to the town Exxon built to house the workers, they needed a refinery and the equipment to extract, crush and dispose of trillions of tons of rock, which cost over $1 billion. So, huge infrastructure costs. In New Jersey, you had hundreds of people researching the process, and on Wall Street, financial analysts were advising Exxon on the numbers. So, huge manpower costs. In the end, Exxon opted to shelve the project, but only after spending US$5 billion on it. It was the company's biggest write-off.[18] That was in the early '80s.

The key to fully unlocking these difficult oil sources is the price per barrel, which will have to rise high enough to justify the costs associated with extracting these more exotic supplies. If in fact we do retrace our steps and start to redevelop shale oil, it will take years and years to produce anything. It's very much like nuclear power, which might take 15 years before you're actually able to turn the lights on as a result of it.

We've extracted a lot of the easy oil around the world over the past 100 or so years and we didn't reinvest in the past 20, so what we're left with is the more expensive stuff. And you're going to have to pay up to get to it. Perhaps even more so as a result of the Gulf spill. You could find headlines from 1979–80, when oil was predicted to go to US$100, US$200 a barrel, and so huge armies of engineers and billions of dollars were put into the search for the next great source. It was fantastical. And it just goes to show what will happen during a boom. When companies start throwing enormous amounts of money at crazy things and the crazy things actually start producing, you know the boom is coming to an end.

Agriculture

It was 1991 when Vinik and I took a trip to Nebraska to learn about farming. Up until then, my notion of a farm was a Halloween pumpkin patch or a six-acre job with a little corn neatly planted in rows and a small red barn. Nebraska was different. It was home to big, industrial-type complexes. Vinik and I were there to learn about and understand the mechanics behind mega-farming. I had two big take-aways from the trip that relate to the agriculture boom and how you'll be able to tell it's nearing an end.

One was that technology plays a big role in agriculture, specifically, when it comes to seeds, soils and fertilizers. It really cannot be understated. We think of technology as the Internet and computer chips, but the type of technological innovation going on in mundane industries like seeds, soils and fertilizers is absolutely essential in understanding how agricultural supply will expand to meet the needs of an increasingly populated industrialized world. Technology is what will allow us to fill the world's pantries and refrigerators with beef, pork, poultry, corn, wheat, rice and soybeans in the coming years. In fact it's the only reason we've been able to stay in the race up until now and feed the millions of new people arriving on the earth every year. It's all technology.

The second big take-away from Nebraska was the importance of mechanized, automated farming. Although they didn't have the same equipment back in the early 1990s, I've seen John Deere presentations in the past couple of years and the new combines, harvesters and other tools of a farmer's trade are something to behold. The tractors alone are unbelievable. They're computer guided so you input your farm layout and a GPS guidance system does the rest. It will harvest based on what's ready to go. It makes the turns in the fields all based on GPS while the farmer's sitting there in an air-conditioned cab listening to Howard Stern on his Sirius Satellite Radio.

Technology and mechanized automation in agriculture are the twin driving forces behind Brazil's success. It was 40 years ago when agronomist Pedro Sanchez visited the country's Cerrado plains. The Cerrado, meaning "closed" or "inaccessible" land, is about 500 million acres in size, or about one-fourth of the continental United States. When Sanchez visited the plains, land sold for US$4 an acre and the only crop that could live in the acidic, infertile soil was dry land rice. The cattle that roamed the plain often fell victim to broken bones from calcium deficiency. Brazil's agriculture minister at the time had invited Sanchez to the Cerrado and asked him if he could make the land productive. Sanchez said yes.[19]

Today, thanks to soil, seeds and fertilizer technology, over 120 million acres of the Cerrado are used for crop production and pastures. This makes it the world's single largest increase in arable land since the American Midwest was settled way back when. Further, another 200 million of the total 500 million acres available is now arable and lies in reserve.[20] As a result of the Cerrado and other projects like it across the vast tropical country, Brazil has turned itself from a food importer to one of the world's great breadbaskets in just over three decades. Between 1996 and 2006, the total value of the country's crops rose from US$23 billion to US$108 billion. Brazil increased its beef exports tenfold in a decade and is now the world's largest exporter and home to the second largest commercial cattle herd (50% larger than the U.S.'s, but smaller than India's) at 170 million head. It is also the world's largest exporter of poultry, sugar cane and ethanol and now accounts for about a third of world soybean exports, second only to America. In terms of grains, Brazilian production has climbed from just under 90 million tonnes in 2000 to 150 million tonnes in 2010.[21] This success is what warranted its inclusion with Russia, India and China as a BRIC and poster boy for global industrialization.

Not surprisingly, John Deere is doing brisk business in Brazil, where arable land now sits 2,000 to 3,000 feet above sea level on top of flat plateaus ideally suited for mechanized, automated farming. The company now has 114 dealers and 140 stores in the country, with plans to add another 60 stores in 2010. In 2007, the company opened a tractor factory in southern Brazil where order books are full for the 310-horsepower, GPS-guided auto-steering tractors.[22]

What lies on the horizon for Brazil and the rest of the world is where we'll take our signal foretelling the boom's end. According to agronomists, the Brazil experiment could be transported to 40% of the world's tropical soils. Latin America alone has over 100 million acres of soil similar to that of the Cerrado. The same goes for large tracts of land in India and many Southeast

Asian countries. In Africa, the countries of Uganda and Kenya are starting to tap the same seed, soil and fertilizer technologies used in Brazil. Technologies, interestingly enough, that were born out of research from the 1950s originally designed to boost yields on Brazil's degraded coffee plantations. At that time, the guys in white lab coats decided to use soybeans, corn and cotton for field trials to speed the coffee research. What they found was that the addition of lime to the soil counteracted toxicity and addressed calcium and magnesium deficiencies.[23]

Fast forward to 1973 when the Brazilian Agricultural Research Corporation, or Embrapa, was formed. Embrapa is a public company that does everything from running a nanotechnology lab to developing new seeds and breeding new types of cattle. Some of Embrapa's achievements that helped turn the Cerrado green include the genetic crossing of African grasses to produce a new variety that produces 20–25 tonnes of grass feed per acre, three times the yield of the original species. This development has helped support the expansion of Brazil's beef herd. Thirty years ago, it took four years to raise a bull for slaughter, but that has been cut to 18–20 months. Embrapa scientists have also bred a bacterium that helps fix nitrogen in legumes, turned soyabeans into a tropical crop and slashed growing periods to allow for two crops a year instead of one. Most recently, Embrapa is experimenting with forest, agriculture and livestock integration. Fields are used alternately for crops and livestock with lines of trees planted in between so cattle can forage.[24]

As promising as it may sound, difficulties abound in countries other than Brazil and these difficulties have nothing to do with soil. Infrastructure such as highways and rail lines are not nearly as well developed in some places as they are in South America's largest country, which means that some farmers are at a disadvantage when it comes to shipping their agriculture commodities. Similarly, irrigation challenges—particularly in Africa— will hamper the cross-pollination of technologies.

Nevertheless, change is afoot and if the advancing technology that has helped Brazil feed an additional 500 million people can be transplanted and multiplied, you'll see agricultural supply making quick gains on growing demands for food. This is especially true in the higher food chain items such as beef, poultry and pork, which are becoming highly sought after.

So the big sign to look for that signals the end of the agriculture boom will be the realization of the ag surge capacity behind the next Brazil. I'm not sure where that will be. But I think it will happen over the next decade or two and feeding the world may not look as daunting as it does now.

The common theme you probably picked up on as I introduced the various signs in gold, oil and agriculture that will foretell the boom's end is the incredible length of time that may be required to ratchet up supply to meet the world's growing demands for these commodities. I do truly believe we will get there. Keep in mind that while change may be slow in coming, when it does occur, it happens quickly. Listen for the fat lady. Further, it's important to remember that these changes might not occur simultaneously. Maybe it starts with oil, maybe gold or maybe agriculture.

And when change arrives, you've got to move down the risk scale. Wherever you are on the risk spectrum, you move down. If you're a huge player with a basket of individual stocks, you might want to consider moving to an asset allocation product. If you're invested in all-equity mutual funds, you may want to consider moving into a balanced product. And if you've got a lot of exposure to gold, oil or agriculture through sector funds, you might want to move to a more diversified fund. The key to taking the risk off is rebalancing. That doesn't mean going to an all-cash portfolio, although at this yet unknown point in time, I suspect cash will start paying something again. Short interest rates will be rising higher than long rates, so owning cash will not be as punitive as it is now.

Other stuff could also be depressed: things like staples, utilities and health care stocks. As Vinik said, the bust will sow the seeds of the next boom.

Endnotes

Chapter 1

1 "China's economic statistics," US-China Business Council, accessed October 19, 2010, http://www. uschina.org/statistics/economy.html.

2 *BRICs Monthly* 10/03 (May 20, 2010): 2, http://www2. goldmansachs.com/ideas/brics/brics-decade-doc.pdf.

3 Ibid.

4 *BRICs and Beyond* (Goldman Sachs Group Inc., 2007), 154, http:// www2.goldmansachs.com/ideas/ brics/book/BRIC-Full.pdf.

5 Aileen Wang and Alan Wheatley, Reuters, "China overtakes Japan as No.2 economy: FX chief," *Financial Post*, July 30, 2010, http://www. financialpost.com/China+overtakes+ Japan+economy+chief/3341189/ story.html.

6 John W. Miller, "China Dethrones Germany as Top Goods Exporter," *Wall Street Journal*, January 6, 2010, http://online.wsj.com/article/ SB126272143898416853.html.

7 "China ends U.S.'s Reign as Largest Auto Market," Bloomberg, January 12, 2010, http://www. bloomberg. com/apps/news?pid=newsarchive &sid=aE.x_r_l9NZE.

8 Spencer Swartz and Shai Oster, "China Tops U.S. In Energy Use," *Wall Street Journal*, July 18, 2010, http://online.wsj.com/article/SB100 01424052748703720504575376712 353150310.html.

9 Aileen Wang and Alan Wheatley, Reuters, "China overtakes Japan."

10 *BRICs Monthly*: 2.

11 *BRICs and Beyond*, 154.

12 *BRICs Monthly*: 2.

13 *BRICs and Beyond*, 120.

14 Ibid., 260.

15 Ibid.

16 Ibid., 261.

17 Ibid.

18 *What I Learned This Week* (newsletter), 13D Research, February 11, 2010: 2.

19 Peter Mathias, *The First Industrial Nation: The Economic History of Britain*, (London: Methuen & Co., 2001), 9.

20 Ibid., 13.

21 Ibid., 4.

22 Dominique N. Khactu, review of *Japan Since 1945: The Rise of an Economic Superpower*, by Dennis B. Smith, *Southern Economic Journal* (January 1, 1997), http:// www.allbusiness.com/specialty-businesses/608537-1.html.

23 *BRICs and Beyond*, 20.

24 "The Squeeze of '79," *Time*, October 22, 1979, http://www.time.com/time/ magazine/article/0,9171,947495,00. html.

25 "Oil Price History and Analysis," WRTG Economics, accessed October 19, 2010, http://www.wtrg. com/prices.htm.

26 Ibid.

27 "Historical World Gold Production," Gold Sheet Mining Directory, accessed October 19, 2010, http:// www.goldsheetlinks.com/production. htm.

[28] Norman N. Bowsher, "Rise and Fall of Interest Rates," *Federal Reserve Bank of St. Louis Review* (August/September 1980): 1, http://research.stlouisfed.org/publications/review/80/08/Rise_Aug_Sep1980.pdf.

[29] "Oil Price History and Analysis," WRTG Economics.

[30] "Historical World Gold Production," Gold Sheet Mining Directory.

Chapter 2

[1] Peter L. Bernstein, *The Power of Gold: The History of an Obsession* (New York: John Wiley & Sons, 2000), 1.

[2] *Encyclopaedia Britannica*, 1970, s.v. "gold."

[3] Peter L. Bernstein, *The Power of Gold*, 1.

[4] Ibid., 25.

[5] Ibid., 167.

[6] Ibid., 203.

[7] Dale Henderson, John Irons, Stephen Salant and Sebastion Thomas, "Can Government Gold be Put to Better Use?" *Federal Reserve International Finance Discussion Papers* 582 (June 1997), http://www.federalreserve.gov/pubs/ifdp/1997/582/default.htm.

[8] "Losing the Midas touch," *The Economist* (US), November 22, 1997.

[9] "Bre-X timeline: From boom to bust," CBC News, July 31, 2007, accessed October 19, 2010, http://www.cbc.ca/news/background/gold/bre-x-timeline.html.

[10] Fabrice Taylor, "A rock-solid case for gold reserves," *Globe & Mail*, November 11, 2009, http://www.theglobeandmail.com/globe-investor/investment-ideas/features/vox/a-rock-solid-case-for-gold-reserves/article1358900/.

[11] *Encyclopaedia Britannica*, s.v. "gold."

[12] Peter L. Bernstein, *The Power of Gold*, 228.

[13] *Encyclopaedia Britannica*, s.v. "gold."

[14] Peter L. Bernstein, *The Power of Gold*, 15–16.

[15] Ibid., 229.

[16] "World Gold Production," Goldsheet Mining Directory, accessed October 19, 2010, http://www.goldsheetlinks.com/production.htm.

[17] Ibid.

[18] Barry Bearak, "South Africa weighs tough mine safety law," *International Herald Tribune*, November 22, 2008.

[19] "Dawn of a New Gold Market —the Washington Agreement," USAGold.com, accessed October 19, 2010, http://www.usagold.com/newgoldmarket.html.

[20] "World gold holdings—volume and value," World Gold Council, accessed October 19, 2010, http://research.gold.org/reserve_asset/.

[21] "World gold holdings—reserve asset statistics," World Gold Council, accessed October 19, 2010, http://research.gold.org/reserve_asset/.

Chapter 3

[1] Jad Mouawad, "Oil," NYTimes.com, March 9, 2009, http://www.nytimes.com/info/oil/ (accessed on October 19, 2010).

[2] Ibid.

[3] *2010 Key World Energy Statistics* http://www.iea.org/textbase/nppdf/free/2010/key_stats_2010.pdf.

[4] *World Oil Outlook 2009* (Vienna: OPEC Secretariat, 2009), 9, http://www.opec.org/opec_web/static_files_project/media/downloads/publications/WOO%202009.pdf.

[5] Ibid., 8–9.

[6] Lester R. Brown, *Outgrowing the Earth* (New York: W.W. Norton & Company, 2004), 23.

[7] "Who Made America? Edwin

Drake," Public Broadcasting Service, accessed October 19, 2010, http://www.pbs.org/wgbh/theymadeamerica/whomade/drake_hi.html.

[8] *Encyclopaedia Britannica*, 1970, s.v. "petroleum."

[9] Steven M. Gorelick, *Oil Panic and the Global Crisis: Predictions and Myths* (Oxford: Wiley-Blackwell, 2010), 70.

[10] "The United States 2007 Review," *Energy Policies of IEA Countries* (Paris: International Energy Agency, 2008), 105, 106, http://www.iea.org/textbase/nppdf/free/2007/us2007.pdf.

[11] "How many Mexicans does it take to drill an oil well?" *The Economist* (US), October 3, 2009.

[12] "How much oil is there in the world?" Organization of the Petroleum Exporting Countries, accessed October 19, 2010, http://www.opec.org/opec_web/en/press_room/179.htm.

[13] *World Oil Outlook 2009*, 10.

[14] "Who Made America? Edwin Drake," Public Broadcasting Service.

[15] *Encyclopaedia Britannica*, 1970, s.v. "petroleum."

[16] Steve Robertson, Georgie MacFarlan, and Michael Smith, "Deep water sector's growth will remain steady through 2010," *World Oil* 227 no. 4 (April 1, 2006), http://www.worldoil.com/April-2006-Deepwater-sectors-growth-will-remain-steady-through-2010.html.

[17] Steven M. Gorelick, *Oil Panic and the Global Crisis*, 70.

[18] Guy Chazan and Jeffery McCraken, "Offshore Brazil Beckons for BP," *Wall Street Journal*, March 10, 2010, http://online.wsj.com/article/SB10001424052748704655004575113991655865532.html.

[19] Steve Robertson, Georgie MacFarlan, and Michael Smith,

"Deep water sector's growth."

[20] "About us," Organization of Petroleum Exporting Countries, accessed October 19, 2010, http://www.opec.org/opec_web/en/17.htm.

[21] Mostafa Zahrami, "The coup that changed the Middle East," *World Policy Journal* 19 no. 2 (Summer, 2002), http://www.jstor.org/pss/40209809.

[22] Guy Chazan, Jeffery McCraken, "Offshore Brazil Beckons for BP."

Chapter 4

[1] "China's Arable Land in Danger of Dropping below Gov't red line," *China Daily*, May 15, 2007, http://www.gov.cn/english/2007-05/15/content_614968.htm (accessed on October 19, 2010).

[2] "Arable land (hectares per person)," World Bank, accessed October 19, 2010, http://data.worldbank.org/indicator/AG.LND.ARBL.HA.PC/countries/1W?display=graph.

[3] Ibid.

[4] Ibid.

[5] *What I learned this week* (newsletter), 13D Research, February 11, 2010: 2.

[6] "Urban population (% of total)," World Bank, accessed on October 19, 2010, http://data.worldbank.org/indicator/SP.URB.TOTL.IN.ZS/countries/1W?display=graph.

[7] Lester R. Brown, *Outgrowing the Earth* (New York: W.W. Norton & Company, 2004), 90.

[8] Joyce Chang, "The Silk Route," *New York Times Magazine*, August 18, 2002, http://query.nytimes.com/gst/fullpage.html?res=9500EFDD103AF93BA2575BC0A9649C8B63.

[9] James Fallows, "China makes, the world takes," *The Atlantic*, July/August 2007, http://www.theatlantic.com/magazine/archive/2007/07/china-makes-the-world-takes/5987/.

10 "How we classify countries," World Bank, accessed October 19, 2010, http://data.worldbank.org/about/country-classifications.

11 *BRICs and Beyond* (Goldman Sachs Group Inc., 2007), 262, http://www2.goldmansachs.com/ideas/brics/book/BRIC-Full.pdf (accessed October 18, 2010).

12 Lester R. Brown, *Outgrowing the Earth* (New York: W.W. Norton & Company, 2004), 44.

13 *BRICs and Beyond*, 262.

14 Lester R. Brown, *Outgrowing the Earth*, 44.

15 Ibid., 89.

16 Ibid., 99.

17 Ibid., 46.

18 "Quarter of US Grain used for Biofuel," E-Energy Market, January 26, 2010, accessed on October 19, 2010, http://www.e-energymarket.com/news/single-view/link//5319e59ab8/article/16/quarter-of-us-grain-used-for-biofuel.html.

19 Lester R. Brown, *Outgrowing the Earth*, 92.

20 Ibid., 91.

21 Ibid., 29, 30, 31.

22 *Encyclopaedia Britannica*, 1970, s.v. "Justus Von Liebig."

23 *Encyclopaedia Britannica*, s.v. "fertilizers and manures: history."

24 Phillip Barak, "Law of the Minimum," University of Wisconsin Department of Soil Science, March 6, 2000, accessed October 22, 2010, http://www.soils.wisc.edu/~barak/soilscience326/lawofmin.htm.

25 *What I learned this week*, 2.

26 *Encyclopaedia Britannica*, s.v. "fertilizers and manures: history."

27 Lester R. Brown, *Outgrowing the Earth*, 65.

28 Fertilizer consumption (kilograms per hectare of arable land)," World Bank, accessed October 20, 2010, "http://data.worldbank.org/indicator/AG.CON.FERT.ZS/countries/CN-IN-R-BU-BR?display=graph.

29 "Mineral Resources of Saskatchewan: Potash," Government of Saskatchewan, accessed October 20, 2010, http://www.er.gov.sk.ca/Default.aspx?DN=3558,3541,3538,3385,2936,Documents.

30 Ibid.

31 *What I learned this week*, 2.

32 "Canada's last hot commodity: Saskatchewan farmland," CBC News, June 20, 2007, http://www.cbc.ca/canada/saskatchewan/story/2007/06/20/farmland-sales.html.

Chapter 5

1 Andrew Ross Sorkin, "Lehman Files for Bankruptcy; Merrill is sold," *New York Times*, September 14, 2008, http://www.nytimes.com/2008/09/15/business/15lehman.html.

2 Andrew Ross Sorkin, "JP Morgan Pays $2 a Share for Bear Stearns," *New York Times*, March 17, 2008, http://www.nytimes.com/2008/03/17/business/17bear.html.

3 Vikas Bajaj, "Stocks Soar on Takeover Plan," *New York Times*, September 8, 2008, http://www.nytimes.com/2008/09/09/business/worldbusiness/09markets.html?fta=y.

4 Andrew Ross Sorkin, "Lehman Files for Bankruptcy."

5 Andrew Ross Sorkin, *Too Big to Fail* (London: Penguin, 2009), 443.

6 *World Economic Outlook Database*, International Monetary Fund, July 7, 2010, accessed on October 10, 2010, http://www.imf.org/external/pubs/ft/weo/2010/01/weodata/index.aspx.

7 Ibid.

8 "Not just straw men: BRICs, emerging markets and the world economy," *The Economist* (US), June 20, 2009 www. highbeam.com/DocPrint. aspx?DocId=1G1:2020018367.
9 Ibid.

Chapter 6
1 Andrew Ross Sorkin, *Too Big to Fail*, (London: Penguin, 2009), 8, 554.
2 "Foreign content rule gets tossed," *National Post*, February 28, 2005, http://www.canada.com/story_print. html?id=8d7911c9-878d-4de5-95e9-67d58dcb81f6.
3 *2009 Year in Review* (Toronto: Investment Funds Institute of Canada Statistics), 5, 6.
4 "U.S. deficit down in first half of 2010: report," Reuters, April 12, 2010, http://www.reuters.com/assets/ print?aid=USTRE63C09I20100413.
5 International Monetary Fund, *The State of Public Finances Cross-Country Fiscal Monitor*, November 3, 2009, http://www.imf.org/external/pubs/ft/ spn/2009/spn0925.pdf.
6 Stephen Jen, "How big could sovereign wealth funds be by 2015," MorganStanley.com, May 3, 2007, accessed October 20, 2010 http:// www.morganstanley.com/views/ gef/archive/2007/20070504-Fri. html#anchored3a90be-419e-11de-a1b3-c771ef8db296.
7 Paul Vieira, "Foreigners buying Canadian securities in record amounts," *Financial Post*, January 19, 2010, http://www2.canada.com/ scripts/story.html?id=2457428.
8 Frank Jack Daniel, "Venezuela to nationalize U.S. firm's oil rigs," Reuters, June 24, 2010, http://www.reuters.com/assets/ int?aid=USTRE65N0UM20100624.

Chapter 9
1 Steven Labaton, "U.S. is taking over a group of banks to head off a run," *New York Times*, January 7, 1991, http://www.nytimes. com/1991/01/07/business/us-is-taking-over-a-group-of-banks-to-head-off-a-run.html.
2 Ben Levisohn, "How should investors play the dollar?" Bloomberg Businessweek, December 17, 2009, http://www.businessweek.com/ print/magazine/content/09_52/ b4161074180150.htm.
3 Wanfeng Zhou, "US dollar share of global reserves slips in Q1," Reuters, June 30, 2010, http:// www.reuters.com/assets/ print?aid=USN3022567120100630.
4 "China should boost gold reserve holdings: media," *China Post*, December 1, 2009, http:// www.chinapost.com.tw/china/ business/2009/12/01/234875/China-should.htm.
5 "World Official Gold Holdings," World Gold Council, September 2010, accessed October 20, 2010, http://www.research.gold.org/ reserve_asset.
6 Ibid.
7 "China should boost gold reserve," *China Post*.
8 Thomas Kutty Abraham and Kim Kyoungwha, "India buys IMF gold to boost reserves as dollar drops," Bloomberg, November 3, 2009, http://www.bloomberg.com/apps/ news?pid=newsarchive&sid=aa6oc6 Wz9Ftg.
9 Javier Bias, "Central banks and investors weigh in as gold market transforms," *Financial Times*, August 17, 2010, http://www.ft.com/ cms/s/0/d627df3c-a9e7-11df-8eb1-00144feabdc0,dwp_

uuid=413b4c2e-b9f8-11dc-abcb-0000779fd2ac.html.

10 Ibid.

11 Ambrose Evans-Pritchard, "Barrick shuts hedge book as world gold supply runs out," *Daily Telegraph*, November 11, 2009, http://www.telegraph.co.uk/finance/newsbysector/industry/mining/6546579/Barrick-shuts-hedge-book-as-world-gold-supply-runs-out.html.

12 Ibid.

13 Pham-Duy Nguyen, "Gold at $2000 becomes inflation-adjusted bullseye for '80 high," Bloomberg, October 18, 2009, http://www.bloomberg.com/apps/news?pid=21070001&sid=a3w9OGzFRe3Y.

14 "Alberta Energy: Facts and Statistics," Government of Alberta, accessed October 20, 2010, http://www.energy.alberta.ca/OilSands/791.asp.

15 "Oil Sands," Canadian Association of Petroleum Producers, accessed October 22, 2010, http://www.capp.ca/canadaIndustry/oilSands/Pages/default.aspx.

16 "Building on sand: Canada's oil boom," *The Economist* (US),

May 26, 2007, http://www.highbeam.com/DOCPrint.aspx?DocId=1G1:163896495.

17 "Alberta's clean energy story," Government of Alberta, accessed October 20, 2010, http://environment.alberta.ca/documents/AB-Clean-Energy-Story.pdf.

18 John S. DeMott, Robert Grieves, and Richard Woodbury, "Energy: Setback for Synfuel," *Time*, May 17, 1982, http://www.time.com/time/printout/0,8816,921222,00.html.

19 Taylor Marcia Zerley, "No bad soils: technology unleashes the tropics for crop production," *Top Producer* (November 1, 2002), http://www.highbeam.com/DocPrint.aspx?DocID=1G1:127974249.

20 Ibid.

21 "The miracle of the cerrado," *The Economist*, August 26, 2010, http://www.economist.com/node/16886442.

22 Taylor Marcia Zerley, "No bad soils."

23 Ibid.

24 "The miracle of the cerrado," *The Economist*.

About the Author

BOB HABER was employed with Fidelity Investments for twenty-four years, culminating with his role as Chief Investment Officer of Fidelity Investment Canada from 1997 to 2009, where he formed Team Canada's research and investment management division. Haber was portfolio manager of both the Fidelity Canadian Disciplined Equity Fund and the Fidelity Canadian Balanced Fund from their inception in September 1998 to March 2009. These funds each earned the prestigious 2009 Canada Lipper Fund Award as the top-performing fund of the decade in each of their respective Lipper categories (Canadian Equity and Canadian Neutral Balanced). Haber is currently an owner of the Boston Celtics basketball team and a member of its Board of Directors, as well as Chief Executive Officer and Chief Investment Officer of Haber Trilix Advisors, LP.